HUSBANDS
Love your Wives

MARVIN A. CARTER

To my Father in Heaven,

may I bring honor to your name

To my father from Heaven,

may I make you proud

Husbands Love Your Wives, by Marvin A. Carter

February 2021
Published by Arcturus Star Publishing,
an imprint of Pink Butterfly Press LLC
www.PinkButterflyPressLLC.com

ISBN#: 978-1-63821-203-4 (paperback)

Table of Contents

Foreword

THE ENGLISH WRITER JAMES RUSSELL Lowell penned these words. "No man can produce great things who is not thoroughly sincere in dealing with himself." When you open this book, be prepared to embark upon a journey that will leave you with the desire to be better. The author performs surgery, opening up his heart and soul to the reader, carefully identifying what has caused both joy and pain in his life. You feel the pressure to live up to expectations, you smile at the small wins and you empathize with the raw truth exposed. Not only an emotional journey, the author engages the reader in a bible study on how to be a better man leading to being a better spouse.

Marvin Carter wrote his personal Psalm 51, we see the confession, the purging, the cleansing, the washing and most importantly the deliverance. One could say that Husbands Love Your Wives is Marvin's Psalm 51:17, "Then I will teach transgressors your ways, so that sinners will turn back to you." Praise God for Marvin trusting God enough to create a blueprint for others based upon his openness and vulnerability. All readers will say, "Thank you!"

Reverend Jamal T. Johnson

Zion Baptist Church

Introduction

It's okay to be scared. Being scared means,
you are about to do something brave.

—The Cuban Guy, *How to Stay Motivated*
During Difficult Times

FOR THOSE WHO ARE NEW to marriage; those in their fifth year or less, welcome to the best and most hardworking club on this side of heaven! These first five years are crucial, you have the grace to fail forward, fall short, and recover. Most importantly, you can know Christ and show perfect love to your spouse. At this point, I say, congratulations and kudos on making it this far! Now you want to learn how to do it better. I am glad you found this resource. Unfortunately, there aren't many handbooks on how to husband correctly but I hope that this will serve as a preliminary resource on your journey.

Now, to the skeptics, the complacent, and to those who believe they have given their best, I offer you a new challenge. Some may view reading this book as a task and ask, "How quickly can I get this done?" I understand that this book might have been a gift. You might approach it like an assignment, and do some of the reading looking for keywords and phrases you can use to prove that you have done your due diligence. It doesn't matter how you found it; *Husbands Love Your Wives* is for you. I am not here to wag a finger at you or hold your feet over a fire. I want you to see this book as an arm over the shoulder or an invitation to the gym or the barbershop where we can be ourselves, while being honest.

Being a husband is both humbling and challenging. It is a great responsibility and that is why this book is titled "Husbands Love Your Wives". It doesn't matter whether you are a seasoned husband or a novice; you must read this book as if you were a blank canvas. Will you be teachable? While I hold a degree in marriage and family therapy, the material here has challenged me too. Of course, we may differ in how we work on our marriages but I urge you to listen. Listen because the principles here are all based on the Word of God. Listen because the worst thing we can do is have it all figured out. My goal is to focus on Christ's example as a husband and promote strategies as to how we husbands' can all do things a bit better. We can be Christ's example to our family, friends, strangers, and, ultimately, the world.

For several years and seasons in my life before writing this book, one scripture unfolded for me each time I read it. The words were penetrating, as if I were reading a letter from my Father. Husbands, love your wives, even as Christ also loved the church, and gave himself for it (Ephesians 5:25, KJV). Seeing those words is like an invitation to God's intentional love, gracious sacrifice, and jubilant expectancy. It amazes me to think of myself as a part of those he wants to delight with his love. You are also one he wants to flood with his abundant love through the sacrifice of Jesus Christ.

So, to you, my brothers in arms and in bond, may you increase daily in Him until you "all reach unity in the faith and in the knowledge of God's Son, growing into a mature man with a stature measured by Christ's fullness (Ephesians 4:13, HCSB). After reading this book, you should be the first one to change, not your spouse. In God's perfect order, the oil of unity will flow from the Father to you and from you through her.

CHAPTER 1

Husbands

The average man fails to realize just how incredibly powerful his everyday actions and attitudes are—especially in the lives of those in his house.

—John Trent, *The Hidden Value of a Man*

THE WORD *HUSBAND* HAS TWO definitions. The first, is a male head of household, while the second definition means to farm or cultivate land. Now, before a picket-sign attack, let's try to break this down into a Twenty-First Century context. This breakdown doesn't completely support marital roles nor does it reinforce the patriarchal ideology that a man must be the breadwinner in the house. It does mean that a husband should be the spiritual leader in the home and a positive contributor in the decision-making process; that is to say, he must be willing to bear the weight of the marital unit's decisions and direction in unity with his wife. God will require you to answer for how you lead your marriage, and eventually, your family.

Before you were married, you weren't pent up in your man cave or parked in front of a television, unless there was something specific on TV that you wanted to see. You were out and about, with wandering eyes and little accountability—and then you married. What became of that man? The desire didn't leave! You chose commitment and singularity. Against the judgment of some and the ridicule of others, you decided to forsake other women to create something beautiful and wonderfully enigmatic. You embarked on a never-ending journey of self-exploration and revelation.

You might not remember all of the details that went into your making that decision, but you chose this life. You decided she was the best thing to happen to you and you couldn't pass her up. You made a vow with confidence that you would "forsake all others" while loving, honoring, and cherishing her. You are a husband. Notice how the journey of husband-hood begins with a series of decisions resulting in these declarations: I do, I will, I am. Those words have or soon will carry more weight than you ever realized.

Marriage doesn't have the power to immediately make men perfect. Like it or not we have history with the idea and roles of marriage. For one man he could have come from a home where marital roles were traditional and love was palpable. While another man could have come from a home where he saw his father mistreat his own wife. That example might lead a man to mistreat his wife in the same way, by expecting her to be his mother, housekeeper, etc. Whether your ideologies on the roles of a husband was formed from family, outside your family or on television, you have a history with it. Unfortunately, in Christianity we have not done an adequate job of teaching the fullness of what it means to be a husband, let alone a man. We rest our laurels on the word's dominion, head of the house, honor, and the like. What's worse is that we've raised generations of men to only know those parts.

To address the elephant in the room, let's be clear: yes, you were given dominion in the garden (Genesis 1:26, KJV), and yes, you are the head of the household. However, neither of these entitle you to be master of the universe. If you dare to say that you are the example of our heavenly husband, who is Christ, but act like a dictator in your home, then you have grossly misunderstood what marriage is. Husbands, at their best, are to be more like the Son than the Father, in that they remain submitted to Him while in relationship with Him. We will discuss submission in another chapter because it requires a lengthier conversation.

Since we've already addressed the first definition of the word *husband*, let's cover the second definition: to cultivate or to till the ground. Cultivation flows immediately after investment. To invest in something means you are opening it up to insert what you have into it. To cultivate is the process of making sure that what you have placed there, grows into its' fullness. Your marriage is a long-term process of investment and cultivation. Standing at the altar is not the fullness of the process, it's only the beginning and so we have work to do. Since many of us are not farmers outside of the occasional cell phone game, we do not know the level of sweat equity that goes into planting and harvesting. I know that many did not know the level of effort it would take to maintain a marriage.

Just like how the conditions of the soil shape a seed's growth, so, too, was your wife shaped by the environment in which she grew up. Until you understand what shaped her, you will never know how to give her what she needs to flourish. I don't just mean big things like traumatic experiences. Consider things like what she cooks, how she punches you in your sleep; how she's influenced by her confidants, or recovers from hurtful feelings. She may have learned to cook because her grandmother took the time to teach her even though the meals were largely unhealthy. She may be extremely resilient as a result of parents who empathized and coached her through disappointments and failures. The idea of investment and cultivation shape the soil of her heart.

3

The best farmers know the land and understand weather patterns and which seeds can handle the climate. When was the last time you cultivated your wife's soil? Cultivation looks different depending on the environment. In some environments the dirt on top has crusted, and it's time to let what is under it breathe; allowing a plant's root system to receive nutrients. In other environments, you can drop a seed right in and let nature take its course. You must keep in mind that any investment in your wife is a seed in the ground. What a task! From time to time, we have to break the ground. Nevertheless, we need to know the type of soil with which we are working. Sometimes you cannot tell what type it is until you try to plant something. When we are examining the soil of her heart, we are looking at the readiness for the seed or the investment. We will look to Christ's parable of the four soils for more insight:

> Then He spoke many things to them in parables, saying: "Behold, a sower went out to sow. And as he sowed, some *seed* fell by the wayside; and the birds came and devoured them. Some fell on stony places, where they did not have much earth; and they immediately sprang up because they had no depth of earth. But when the sun was up, they were scorched, and because they had no root they withered away. And some fell among thorns, and the thorns sprang up and choked them. But others fell on good ground and yielded a crop: some a hundredfold, some sixty, some thirty (Matthew 13:3-8, NKJV)."

One of the original purposes and definition of a husband is to work the ground. Inside of each of you biologically, spiritually and metaphorically are seeds that God has given you specifically for your wife. If you look at how you both have what each other needs that is not by accident. The reciprocity of your marriage is a mirror of a farmer and the soil. As you invest in her she yields infinitely more.

As a single man, you grew as much as you were designed to, then united your path with another's in holy matrimony. While the choice was ultimately yours in who you would marry, the person you chose agreed to the investment. So, on your wedding day, at the altar, you stood there, full of hope and ready to sow. In the initial stages you sowed into your wife as you saw other men invest in their wives, in good and bad ways. You tried everything; using your strength and knowledge, gifts, showering her with compliments and unsolicited opinions, but the results still left you both feeling like you need more. You don't see her changing to *your* fantasy as quickly as you would have hoped and you become frustrated because you don't feel effective.

"What is her soil truly asking for?" you might ask. "This is too much." The ground is begging for the seed from the hands of one who studies the soil of her heart!

I know what you're thinking now: how do I learn the soil of her heart? First, you ask God who formed her. She longs for elevation in His Word—in fact, everything she needs is in His Word! Does this mean you quote scriptures to her before a moment of passion? Not quite. Pastor Jasper T. Daniels III says, "the Word of God in its most basic form is God's opinion about any given situation, purpose, or consequence."

How did God feel about creation? God said it was good. How does God feel about coming second in your life? He says not to put anything before Him. What does God think about you even in the lowest points of life? The response is, "I know the plans I have for you, of good and not of evil, to give you a future and a hope (Jeremiah 29:11, KJV)." Now, what is God's opinion of your wife? When the scripture talks about the sower sowing the Word, it means sowing what God deems important instead of our feelings. How do we build our spouses in the Word? By learning her soil type, so that our words might take root.

Jesus tells us of different ground types in his parable of the four soils. We can use this as a framework to understand how words might be received and how to cultivate the best from our marriages.

The Wayside

The phrase *fell by the wayside* suggests that something was forgotten or failed to succeed. The wayside is the type of soil that does not receive the word. Instead, it leaves it where it fell. In other words, any seed that is sown takes no root and bears no fruit. It doesn't bear fruit because of the hardness of the ground. As a result, the evil one can come and steal away what was about to be planted.

It took quite a while to understand how this ground actually worked in the context of marriage. While writing this section, the Holy Spirit whispered three words to me, "I'll never let." I'm sure you've heard it before within and outside of your marriage. "I'll never let another person hurt me like that again." "I'll never lend money to my family." "I'll never trust a prophet ever again" are a few examples of phrases that precede hard heartedness. Some underlying emotions to recognize include disappointment, shame, embarrassment, ridicule, etc. When you attempt to sow into your wife with the Word of God, she can't receive it because, out of her own mouth, she has hardened that place. The Bible shows that human hands can't remedy hard heartedness. God has to bring healing and new life as promised in Ezekiel 36:26 (NIV) I will give you a new heart and put a new spirit in you; I will remove from you, your heart of stone and give you a heart of flesh. You should commit specific prayers to these areas in both of your hearts so that you can be in a place to give and receive.

In marriage counseling, they asked us to discuss our views on money and our debt. I wasn't honest about how much I had in student loans and it almost destroyed our union before it even began. As a result, my wife who was previously married, began to rehearse that she would never let anyone put her in financial strain again. What followed was almost a year of struggle around the idea of unity with our finances. I wanted everything in the open and she was keeping enough tucked away just in case things went south. During that time, I couldn't just beat the ground, hoping that it would give way. I had to be transparent about any money transactions I made because I knew I was a good steward of money but plagued by student loan debt. Then, one day my wife woke up and said, "this is really hard for me but I think God is leading me to put it all on the table and show you everything." I was floored. It wasn't about seeing the money she stashed. For me, it was the fact that my honesty, coupled with trusting in God's word led to Him softening her heart. Men, you can argue and fight about it all day but her soil is not always fertile. Your responsibility is to steward the area of hard heartedness in a way that creates the landing spot for God. When He breaks up the ground, your stewardship signals to your wife that she can trust you in this area without regret.

Stony Ground

We have all been in a conversation where we feel we gave someone wisdom gems. Those gems came at a high cost and you handle with great honor. With your heart ready to give, they leave your mouth and land to the receipt of great excitement. After which, you learned they did the exact opposite of your suggestion; how infuriating. The stony ground gives all appearance that you have been effective but it yields no fruit.

Stony ground speaks of soil in the heart that keeps everything at the surface level. It's taken as good advice or as someone trying to voice concern without upsetting the applecart. The issue such a viewpoint present is that you do not take any ownership of what was being given. The enthusiasm, then withers away at the first sign of trouble and the seed follows. One warning in the observation of the verse is the perception that the stony ground was viable. A good husband marks the area where there seems to be no root.

Consider this example: a husband and his wife are talking about getting healthier. The husband is adamant about the way they repair disagreements. He even cites that other's opinions have gravely influenced their ability to come to an agreement. The cycle, to this point, was to wait long enough until his wife was hungry and use that to get in her good graces. The issue never reached resolution; instead, it is buried only to find itself useful again. As he attempts to lead his wife by showing her how the enemy uses others to bring disunity between them and they end up going to bed mad. He even points her to scriptures about why it's not good for their marriage (Romans 16:17, NIV & Ephesians 4:26, KJV). She may be excited about bringing more unity until separation from those voices feels like the abandoning of the friendship and they continue to go to bed mad at each other. The heat from her friends can act as the sun to scorch the seed.

When the environmental pressures come against your marriage, have you worked on removing the barriers so that you can sow the Word to great effect? Gentlemen, this is hard work and 'heartwork.'

Thorny Ground

The thorny ground can be confusing because the focus here is solely on how the ground responds to the seed. Notice that the verse did not say the seed grew, it said the thorns grew. The growth of the thorns shows you that the field had a different kind of seed that kept anything good from growing. Thorny soils are among the hardest for anyone to get through, even counselors. Thorns are boundaries around raw areas of our lives, guarding our vulnerabilities against anyone or anything that are observed and labeled as 'intruders'. What are the spikes covering? Remember, thorns start as seeds, too. The fact that thorns are present indicates that the soil was able to produce which points to good ground!

Jesus says something similar in Matthew 13:24-25 (KJV), "The kingdom of heaven may be compared to a man who sowed good seed in his field, but while his men were sleeping, his enemy came and sowed weeds among the wheat and went away." Jesus's words show a hit-and-run attack on good soil! We could quickly point to the 'who' but we should be more concerned with what was sown. When we focus on what was sown, we take power away from those who wanted to cause harm and place our focus on the God who protects us and watches over our covenant.

What was sown in that once good ground and how long has it been there? How deep are the roots? What have these thorns choked out? What is a husband's responsibility to do about them? Those thorns are hopes and dreams that were thought to be dead. Broken confidence, naive beliefs, and faulty belief systems, are in there as well to name a few. According to the book *35 Dumb Things Well-Intended People Say*, many of us create barriers or distance between ourselves and others to save ourselves from incurring more pain. Some men uncover those areas while dating and others stumble upon those barriers months or years into the marriage. You know when you have encountered one of those areas in several ways: your partner shuts down unexpectedly, there is an adverse reaction to a perceived normal interaction, or there is a noticeable change in the atmosphere. Your response must be to prayerfully; consider what the issue might have been and make space for the conversation.

Thorny grounds encompass a myriad of areas, many of which are taboo to talk about in open conversation. With topics ranging from familial sexual trauma secrets, emotional abuse, self-harm, addictions, etc. these areas are difficult to navigate even for the most seasoned of counselors. When you take the time to listen, she will uncover those areas and issues in her own time and you have to be patient. If you have areas that are protected by thorns this can serve as a powerful opportunity to go to God together about the details and seek Him for direction in how to be restored in that area. Thorns don't need to be cut down; they need to be pulled out by the root system. Once you identify symptoms, you may need to collaborate with a counselor, pastor, or family to find the underlying cause of it for you both. Do not take this area lightly! Whatever you won't uproot will cause more pain down the road!

Good Ground

Good ground is a part of the allure of marriage. When we see unions we want to emulate, it is likely because the couple is in harmony. They look good together and they feed off each other's palpable energy. You can recognize the passion, intimacy, and transparency because they are seemingly all given and received with grace, love, and peace. This is the soil where a seed comes back to you more robust and vibrant after you put it in the ground. Like a grape seed in the field, starting small but transforming into a heavily laden vine. Planting seeds of hope, safety, belief, and love into your wife pays off sevenfold. She yields fruit in the form of homemaker, best friend, business partner, counselor, and so much more! Good ground doesn't return a seed for a seed. It always multiplies the efforts of the sower.

God told Adam, the first man, that as punishment for his sin, he would only produce by the sweat of his brow, and since that time, we have had to become soil specialists. The best husbands are the ones who learn how and when to plant a seed. A good sower knows how to prepare the harvest for the seasons to come. We have all gone through or will go through seasons where it seems like nothing we do is good enough, recognized, or supported. Good and honest communication assists us in getting through those times. Good ground is a bulwark against rough seasons that may not feel like it's producing a good harvest. In Genesis 41, Joseph prepares the land for the impending famine, capitalizing on the timing of the good ground and as a result, it saved the nation. John Gottman calls the investment that protects against future issues an "emotional bank account." The emotional bank account thrives when you make more deposits than withdraws. It proves its worth in disagreements because when you have more in the bank when issues come your partner has a history of how you have made positive deposits that fight the negative thoughts that plague each of us when we are in conflict with our partners.

After the fall, everything Adam attempted to produce via a seed took sweat equity. Can you imagine what it must have been like to wait for the first planted seed to grow? Many of us today might have dug up the seeds and planted them on different soil, hoping for progress to occur. Well, men, if you've ever prayed for patience, you are living in God's answer. As husbands, and self-proclaimed fixers, we often want to find the shortest solutions to even the most significant problems. James 5:7 (NIV) points to an illustration of a farmer waiting for the land to yield its valuable crop, through all of the seasons. It's quite simple, there are no shortcuts in cultivating a solid, God centered marriage. After all, you do not solve famine with a grain of wheat, nor can you solve years of experience with a compliment, a gift, or a nice dinner; all of those things are types of investments. The process of producing a desired result can be laborious but you will need perseverance because the process can be a bit bumpy.

The nature of a husband and a seed are identical. Both are disruptive to a culture and environment. Have you ever thought of your husbandry as disruptive? To cultivate good soil, you have to be willing to disturb the ground; to fight against the statistics of divorce, you have to be ready to go to lengths of vulnerability that are disruptive for you and your wife. A myth about good marriages is that they have no disagreements or arguments. There is a way to disagree with your spouse and still break ground for seeds. Even in disagreement, you both can grow together! In essence, we are always investing into the hard, to break three strong cords (Ecclesiastes 4:12, KJV).

Here's how it works: you submit to God and she submits to God in your personal walks. Then, you both submit to each other in love. Every farmer has an obligation and a desire to the seed, to see beyond the kernel to its fullness. There isn't a farmer alive today or in history who plants a seed hoping for nothing to grow. Therefore, you must sow good seed, expecting a harvest. Ecclesiastes 11:6 (NIV) says, "Sow your seed in the morning, and at evening let your hands not be idle, for you do not know which will succeed, whether this or that, or whether both will do equally well." While Galatians 6:9 (AMP) says Let us not grow weary or become discouraged in doing good, for at the proper time we will reap, if we do not give in. When you have good ground, you need to be liberal in sowing! That means every chance that you get, regardless of how motivated you feel, seed into your wife. Sow every principle of the word of God that you can, talk about unity, beauty, passion, forgiveness, stewardship, and sonship. As you sow liberally, don't look for immediate harvest or fruit but trust that God, "the Lord of the Harvest" (Matthew 9:38, KJV) will bring the fruit of your labors at the proper time. You may never be able to pinpoint exactly when but your consistency and patience will yield exponentially!

In our first year of marriage, my wife was feeling down because she had a lull in her business. She thought she was losing momentum and that her creativity was at an all-time low. This loss of energy and creativity made her reflect on other times where she wasn't successful and she began to doubt herself. For weeks I encouraged her only with words as best as I knew how. Nothing was able to sustain a smile on her face and that hurt me deeply. Her friends would encourage her in many ways, some saying exactly what I said, and I fell into the trap, "I just told you that, but all right." I admit, I did not steward that seed well. Everything I did hit stones or landed by the wayside or so I thought.

When I finally submitted my way to His will, I asked God how I could help her. Then suddenly, while driving, the thought hit me of a creative visualization that I had never imagined. I went to Walmart and excitedly bought supplies. Our living room was going to resemble a detective's workroom. It would be a crazy sight and I couldn't have been more excited!

Two days later, I woke her up to the sound of soft music playing and invited her downstairs. I was brimming with excitement but needed to pace myself so she could soak up all of my creativity, which was actually obedience. I reminded her of the words God spoke to her about who she was in his eyes. Then, I poured confidence back into her with some life verses she has always kept close. One of those scriptures was the story of Esther and the apex of the story came in a single line, "For if you remain silent at this time, relief and deliverance for the Jews will arise from another place, but you and your father's family will perish. And who knows but that you have come to your royal position for such a time as this (Esther 4:14)?" She needed to know that she was necessary for this time and had not run her full race! The words I sowed into her that day helped her to look at her destiny and not the appearance of delay. To follow Christ and not to trust in her own creative juices. In the moment, she was not as wowed as I would have imagined. I encouraged myself that I was a sower; I couldn't possibly expect a tree in that brief span of time.

Several months later, my wife registered her non-profit organization. It created streams of influence and income that would never have been there if I had not seized the opportunity to sow into my wife at the level of her need with God's word. I knew a failure to seize the opportunity to do so would have increased the already palpable frustration. Even more deeply than that, I felt called to sow in good ground.

The Bible is clear that if you sow seeds sparingly you will reap sparingly and if you sow bountifully you will reap bountifully (2 Corinthians 9:10). In other words, if you generously sow God's word, your time, attention, and love into your wife you will never find lack in your marriage. To those of you who purpose to be a husband who sows willingly we know that God wants to prosper us even in our marriage. It's not likely that the perfect condition to sow may ever present itself to sow into your wife so take every occasion to do so. You sow the Word and let God do the work.

How and what are you sowing into your wife's dreams and purpose? How are you sowing into what God wants from your marriage?

CHAPTER 2

Husbands Love

> *What you are afraid to do is a clear indica-*
> *tion of the next thing you need to do.*
>
> —Ralph Waldo Emerson

THE BEST WAY TO THINK about love in the context of being a husband is not as an object you can pick up and put down at your leisure. The love I'm talking about is so much more than a situational tool in your tool bag. Do you remember the bag Mary Poppins carried? She carried a bag where she always had what was necessary for the situation. It was seemingly bottomless. Now, if you've seen some of the handbags that are out today, this isn't too far-fetched an idea.

If we were to imagine how we love and honor our wives fitting into a bag, would it be deep or shallow? Would it be full of new ideas or simply recycling the old faithfuls? I understand that we can't always come up with something new, but as husbands we have to lean into the creativity of God. Think of this, when God shows us His passion for us through favor, grace, and mercy, it never looks the same every time. Some examples of God's love and concern for us are how: He sent ravens to a starving prophet, and Jesus fed five thousand people with five loaves of bread and two fish. God sent food to an entire nation daily for their gathering, and Jesus visited His disciples to show Thomas that he didn't forget about him.

In the present day, there are times where his favor helps you in ways you don't necessarily qualify for, like deals or discounts or the ultimate never-ending example of love in His forgiveness. God's grace and mercy are extensions of his ever-present, deep, and abiding love for us. The Apostle John discusses this in the conclusion of his epistle, "Jesus did many other things as well. If every one of them were written down, I suppose that even the whole world would not have room for the books that would be written (John 21:25, KJV).

Don't you wish for the testimony of your wife to be: "I could not tell you all of the amazing things that he has done for me! If I wrote them down it could fill more books than we could ever read," I know I would! As husbands, we must break the dimly lit mirror and closely examine how we are showing our love to our wives consistently and creatively.

Loving our wives as Christ loves His church is more than being a "one-trick pony." God's love for us is anything but one-dimensional; it is vast and unexplainable. Your love for your wife has to be as passionate as Christ's love for the lost. It should vary in such a way that she can never pinpoint where it will end or when it begins. Yet, it should be so intentional that she always feels like your favorite; your one and only. This is how you meet her needs and exceed her hopes.

Most often, we allow the combination of situations and reactions to drive us to transactional love. There, we fall painfully short of Christ's example of love. Whereas you might perform a thoughtful task in love, instead you wait for your wife to prove herself worthy of your love. She must initiate and you respond. Brothers, if Christ is our example, He never waited for us to do anything before He showed us his love. He went first. A husband's love must be selfless, consistent, creative, and intentional. As an underlying current your love must be communicated in every way imaginable, just like Christ's does. Regular communication consists of combinations of verbal and nonverbal communication. What you say is only marginally important to what you are communicating.

Many of us have sat with other husbands, listened to podcasts, or even attended seminars where men have told us how to communicate with our wives. As helpful as those things were, the best that information could do was provide a formula with variables. You would plug those generic variables into the equation based on what you knew about your wife. While they may have discussed how to fix your miscommunication issues, at the root they were trying to get you to see how important it was to communicate love and care to your wife.

As many can attest, love is hard to quantify numerically and even harder to qualify where it comes from or how it makes us feel. It would take you no time at all to Google the word *love*. You would come up with more than a million hits on what love is, and what it isn't including all of the shortcuts to perfection. You would see the top 25 ways to show love, 30 new techniques to ravishing love, and more. I would hazard to guess that no less than 100-million times, the question "what is love?" or "how do I know that I'm in love?" has been researched on various search engines. Even as I type these words, an advertisement for a college dating app flashes across the television screen! Simply put, everyone is looking for love.

Let's break down exactly what love is. In doing so, it's important to know that love comes in different forms. Most notably, philosophers in ancient Greece put love into four categories: storge, phileo, eros, and agape. I'll discuss them here but I recommend that you read C.S. Lewis's The Four Loves for deeper understanding. The following definitions are taken from C.S. Lewis' The Four Loves.

Storge- Affection; love that derives from family and are naturally developing familiar, affectionate bonds between them

Philia/Phileo- friendship, love between friends

Eros- "Being in Love" but can be reduced to a raw "appetite" for pleasure. It can mature and become a gateway to greater intimacy

Agape- Love that is unconditional based on the person as an image bearer of Christ; love of God.

With the basic understanding of these more common terms, we have laid a framework through which we can understand. As a husband attempting to pattern himself after the example of Christ, how we love is an amalgamation of the four loves being anchored and garnished by Agape love. For example, you can have an abiding friendship with your wife that feels extraordinarily familiar. It would seem as if you have known each other for years, that's Philia. All the while you may experience emotions of being in love, sexually attracted and sharing with her the love of God. If we only operate well in the romantic love, eros, but fail in the unconditional, we are only partially operating, which is to say, we are struggling. As you read the following sections it is the hope that you would see all of these loves as action items that we can work on. Jesus models each one of them individually and collectively so you can know, it's possible!

Consistent Love

You must reconcile with yourself that you are a creature of habit. Likely, you have a Monday-through-Friday routine that doesn't change much. This means if you are not careful, you could go through your week without much thought—like you were on autopilot.

Autopilot requires only moderate course corrections, and it does not matter who is in the copilot slot to function. Being the head of your house and a true husband means you can't be on autopilot, and treating your marriage like this is dangerous and foolish. It assumes that she will notify you when you need a course correction in enough time to avoid her being upset and for you to refocus and re-engage.

While autopilot seems like a great idea, we forget something important about it; it cannot account for turbulence. When turbulence hits your marriage, the knee-jerk reaction is to take back the controls and strong-arm them to avoid collisions. That "formula" of buying gifts, apologizing profusely, and promising to change has worked before with the expectation that, like last time, everything will be okay. The formula, in varying degrees, might work for months or years, but eventually, it will yield a different, more turbulent response from her. For example, if an apology, a promise to be different, and roses follow each rough spot in your marriage, it will get old relatively quickly. We see this most often when our wives tell us that they need more attention, a date, or even a vacation with just the two of you.

The advice of many seasoned couples is "never stop dating." They have set schedules and block the time for just them amidst the hustle of professional life and busy schedules. My wife and I set up a "one date a month" rule, and we have stuck to it. We label our plans as "the date" and I would feel like a proud peacock of a husband; I was "meeting my wife's needs" or so I thought. The problem was that while I was consistent in keeping to the "one date a month" rule, I became a Pharisee to our covenant marriage. I was offering lip service and following the law of our agreement, but I missed the heart of the issue we created the rule to protect.

Doing the minimum kept us from arguing for a while, but the minimum did not fill my wife's emotional cup. Whatever it accomplished didn't last long. She had every right to be upset because my heart was not in it. Now, I have laid on the landmine for you and you should examine if your heart is in everything you do for your wife. Is your 'doing' an extension of your love or simply a vapor of it? Was Jesus words reinforced by action or were his words full but his actions empty? Christ didn't love His creation because he did things for them. He worked miracles because he loved them. When every action is done from the true place of love, we can move past checkboxes and fear of negative consequences to creating deep trust and bustling romance.

Can your wife trust you to do what you said you would do every time? Even Horton the Elephant stood by his mantra, "I meant what I said, and I said what I meant. An elephant's faithful, one hundred percent!" I don't need to be a prophet to tell you that she will assess you for your consistency in every area of your life together. If you only do tasks when she asks you to or if you feel motivated to act after an argument so that you can "shut her up," or tune out when the conversation requires you to be vulnerable, you are getting negative marks. Consistency requires being present in the moment, in her feedback and criticism, and in making up. Without said consistency, she will feel undervalued and unappreciated, which is the last thing you want.

Present Love

One of the worst feelings, if not the worst feeling in any relationship, is feeling like you are in it alone. That lonely feeling could mean that one or both partners are absent emotionally, physically, mentally or spiritually. As relationships are already a risky endeavor, no one goes into it believing that they would have to do it alone.

The prophet Isaiah stated that the Savior would have a name, Emmanuel, God with us (Isaiah 7:14, KJV) and the psalmists wrote that, "God is our refuge and strength, a very present help in the time of trouble (Psalm 46:1, KJV). Then the Apostle Paul writes, "we do not have a high priest who is unable to sympathize *and* understand our weaknesses *and* temptations, but One who has been tempted [knowing exactly how it feels to be human] in every respect *as we are...* (Hebrews 4:15, AMP)." Altogether, they show us Jesus as present in the midst of all issues.

The story of the 'Three Hebrew Boys in the Fiery Furnace' is a Bible story staple where we emphasize that God is there no matter what the trial. That is the point. When we begin to deeply and passionately love and lead our wives; we can't sit outside of every situation, viewing it objectively. There are some days where our wives are excited and you have to put your fatigue to the side to celebrate with her. When she is scared, we take the moments to reassure her. When she just needs a big hug to let her know she won't have to carry all of the burden alone, we pull her close and hold her. Being present doesn't have to be grandiose but it does need to be felt. Love that is present helps her to fight feelings of isolation. She doesn't want to go to someone else to make her feel alive, heard, seen, or otherwise.

Jesus modeled what many men fail to develop, that's empathy. With the woman at the well, Jairus' and his daughter, and those whom he healed he showed great empathy and compassion. Now to you, you have the ability to be empathetic but you are just un-practice. He took the time to ask questions and listen. He took the time to understand their pain and respond. Similarly, we have to be willing to sit in the problem with her, as we would expect God to be there when we have issues, as He promised. Some things your wife may go through could make you feel helpless, "what do I do", you might ask. I implore you to be like Christ and be present with her. Being present increases trust; it increases hope that it will get better, and gives her confidence that you'll be there when it matters the most.

Love her with your Mind

As men, we can be awfully single minded, can't we? Essentially, how can we get from point A to point B the fastest? Things that interrupt that flow never get our full attention. Instead, we give it just enough to settle the immediacy and resume what we were doing before. We can be having a conversation with our wife while our minds are somewhere else. Why is it so easy to be absent from the moments that matter most? Do you get distracted and tune others out often? Does it happen when your boss calls you into their office? Does it happen when your favorite team is playing? Ironically, the answer is most likely no. When you first started checking out of conversations, you might find that it was a defense mechanism. If you can't hear the verbal onslaught you can walk away with your emotions intact. However, checking out seems disrespectful. Checking out seems to say what I can create in my mind is more important than what's happening in front of me. How do you remain present in those moments? Like a wild horse that has gotten loose, it is the responsibility of the ranch hand to corral the horse. That is essentially what the Apostle Paul meant by bringing every thought into subjection or under control to make it obedient to Christ (2 Corinthians 10:5, KJV). Any thoughts that cause you to fall out of unity with your covenant partner has to be brought into subjection.

To be clear, there is nothing wrong with having an imagination or daydreaming, timing is key here. When used to create distracting space between you and your wife, during a conversation or moments requiring your attention, they are dangerous. You take what should be a time of sharing, intimacy, and growth and exchange it for a picture that you have manipulated. It points to the idea that when you daydream during a conversation, it might mean that you feel like you are losing the ability to feel in control and so your mind creates the narrative that you can do just that.

Communicative Love

In any relationship's hierarchy of needs, communication is the base and pinnacle. Communication serves as an entryway to empathy, intimacy, and the exit door from misunderstanding. A podcast that I listen to frequently, *Real Men Connect* changed my perspective on the importance of communication. If I asked you, what are commonly called the top three reasons for divorce you might name money, lack of intimacy, and failure to communicate. Darius Carter, founder of Prosperity College, which helps families, learn financial literacy and gain financial freedom broke down why money is not the root cause for marital failure. He went on to say that, "communication is the number one reason for divorce, because incomplete communication on any part of marriage leads to failure in every part."

The conversations you willingly choose not to have; contribute to the arguments you most certainly will have in the future. Furthermore, it adds to the mental anguish we go through afterward; our confidence comes under fire quickly followed by heartless efforts, our lack of attention, and eventually crossing our boundaries. Some, if not a majority, of the battles we fight within our marriage are conversations we do not know how to articulate because we do not practice how to communicate due to the fear that something may be taken away if we do.

Think back to the last disagreement you had with your wife. Did you listen more or talk more? Did you understand her heart or did you argue the "facts"? Did you find ways to race to humility or did you stand on the proverbial high ground erect trophies to your rightness, demanding she bow to you? "Be swift to hear and slow to speak, slow to anger, slow to wrath (James 1:19, KJV)" is undoubtedly easier said than done. Grace filled communication becomes paramount to decreasing the frequency and intensity of disagreements. Consistent, healthy communication boosts connectedness and solidifies their identity as someone you value.

When Christ walked the Earth, he grew his following by being transparent and being highly communicative about his heart for humanity. Even today, the heart of Jesus is seen through his Word as is his desire for his bride. Similar to Christ, we also have hopes and dreams for a bright future with our brides.

From the blessed hope of a long life together, learning and understanding each other even down to our smallest quirks and to having a strong, consistent connection to each other that insulates us from the barrage of distractions against it.

We are called to be as Christ is to His church, and that means we must become proficient communicators even when doing so is uncomfortable. To achieve this, we must do the following: recognize your wife's need for safety even within your conversation, contribute to the building of her faith and collaboratively create a space where truth is paramount. By now you have already understood that it is what you say and how you say it. The consequence of open, graceful, and intentional communication is growth with each other and in God. You become more mature and reflect the mature gospel of Jesus Christ" (Ephesians 4:15, KJV).

How Do I Explain All of This?

Looking at Maslow's Hierarchy of Needs, we see safety second only to our most basic human need of food, water, and shelter. God provides us protection in His Word and our relationship with Him. Jesus always spoke about safety in the form of houses or places. For example,

"And if I go and prepare a place for you, I will come again and receive you to myself; that where I am, there you may be also (John 14:3 (KJV))." He wanted the church to know that in Him, you have a place of rest, safety, and security. Not just a physical space, but a space where we can be without fear of ridicule or judgment for our current state.

Likewise, your wife needs to have a place where she can be herself without fear. If she does not feel safe during your conversations, then home is not a true place of safety. It doesn't matter how well you provide for her materially. A safe home operates without any abuse: physical, mental, emotional, spiritual, or social. She should not feel manipulated or coerced, because she is a free moral agent as all people are. The invitation to be with Christ was a free and open invitation to relationship and intimacy. Can you say the same about your home and your conversations with your wife?

Acknowledge that your communication is what you say and how you are saying it. You are to edify her.

"For no man ever yet hated his own flesh; but nourisheth and cherisheth it, even as the Lord the church (Ephesians 5:29, KJV). "Let no corrupt communication proceed out of your mouth, but that which is good to the use of edifying, that it may minister grace unto the hearers (Ephesians 4:29, KJV)."

I know you have good intentions at the start of a conversation, you're just bringing something up that you have held in for a while. You deliver it haphazardly, and *bam!* An argument ensues. If we take a step back, we could pick apart the delivery, the environment, or the tone but the issue predates the delivery. Before you start talking about the issue, ask yourself, am I bringing this up because I want my wife to hurt as I am hurting? Am I using this conversation to grow in unity with her? Will my words leave her built up or broken down? A key component to the first question requires you to know yourself and be in touch with how you are truly feeling. The key to the second is learning to quiet yourself long enough to hear her heart. Lastly, if your conversation leaves your wife feeling beat up you have missed the edification portion. To edify means to improve morally and/or intellectually but also spiritually. In order to edify your wife, you must ask yourself how you can contribute to her growth. While you are not the author nor finisher of her faith, your responsibility is to build her up.

Honesty, Even When It Hurts

"Wherefore putting away lying, speak every man truth with his neighbor: for we are members one of another (Ephesians 4:25 (KJV))."

Good friends know that after they have spoken honestly with one another, they will likely remain friends. It can be easy to forget that you dated before you were married, and before that you may have even been friends. There were no vows on that friendship yet, your devotion and honesty were hand-in-hand. For whatever reason, marriage seems to make some people cowardly and fragile, which creates dissatisfaction, or worse. The old adage suggests that familiarity breeds contempt.

If you can't be honest with your wife, you might be treating her as a parent, a supervisor, or an enemy, which makes you a child, a worker, or an enemy. Dishonesty is a telltale sign that pride is in operation. Robbing your partner of the truth is the furthest thing from the character of Christ who identifies Himself as, "the Way, the Truth, and the Life (John 14:6, KJV)." Telling lies or operating with dishonesty undermines the very model of loving your wife as Christ loved the church.

If you feel like you have to lie to keep the peace, that is not love; it's fear. We know that the one who fears is not yet made perfect in love (1 John 4:18, KJV). While honesty isn't always easy and it may not put a smile on either of your faces, you effectively win the battle against fear and pride simultaneously.

Don't Listen Only to Respond. You are Her Confidant.

Listen before you speak, for to speak before you've heard the facts [is stupid] and will bring humiliation"
—(Proverbs 18:13, (The Passion Translation).

"In all thy getting, get understanding" (Proverbs 4:1b).
Have you ever been in a conversation with someone who only listens to half of what you say because they spent the majority of the time waiting to respond with their quickly crafted response? Then, as if you weren't already insulted by having to repeat yourself, they ask questions you already answered in your statement? In doing so, they dismiss the connectedness of your thoughts and emotions while puffing themselves up into believing that they figured it out even before you finished. In my experience, they are never close to the right answer. If you are guilty of this, you ignore the emotional reach, while destroying future opportunities for vulnerability. When anyone within a relationship feels they can't be themselves, exposed, and raw they lose trust in the relationship. The capacity for that relationship to grow shrinks until the safety returns.

As a preconceived notion of marriage our spouses trust that they can come to us and offload some of those emotional burdens without the fear that we will spend our time sifting through for solutions. If you are listening to respond, refute, or interject, you could be missing the real issues. A true confidant is someone who can stand and walk beside you when you're in pain, but who doesn't need a say to feel validated. Moments like that are emotional support opportunities that we so often miss because we "see the solution" even before we hear the end of the matter. However, those emotions need a safe place just to be. To her, that is paramount to the solution. When we listen, we give our spouse a place to unload, and simultaneously, we learn her triggers, what attacks her confidence, where she feels unsupported, or how she is feeling beyond the busyness of a daily routine. The confidant role provides her space to be understood and vulnerable in her thoughts and emotions.

Invite the Holy Spirit into the Conversation.
You are Both Children of God.

> *Likewise, the Spirit helps us in our weakness. For we do not know what to pray for as we ought, but the Spirit himself intercedes for us with groanings too deep for words.*
> —(Romans 8:26 (ESV).

Inviting the Holy Spirit into the conversation is easier said than done. However, partnering with the Holy Spirit helps us get through tough conversations. Once, after a heated discussion with my wife about what support looks like for her, I left the house and went for a run. In an attempt to clear my head and reset, I found myself replaying the argument over and over. The Holy Spirit interrupted my thoughts and showed this example: "Like a quarterback and a coach, after the quarterback has thrown an interception, you come to the sidelines to review the play. Yeah, your ego gets hurt when you see what you could have done better, but in your next series, if you take heed to the words I say, it will create a path to success for you."

I was dumbfounded because it was so simple. The Holy Spirit highlighted at that moment that I shut Him out of my heart because I figured I could do this one on my own. He said, all I had to do was hear my wife's heart instead of attempting to justify my being right. She wanted to know I was on her side, in her corner, and had her back. I could have made a game plan about what that would look like later. In that moment, she needed my support.

The Holy Spirit is not just your comforter but also, your wife's as well, serving as both advisor and mediator. The Spirit helps us in our weakness. In our marriage sometimes, our weakness is focusing on our own needs and desires so intensely that we neglect those of our partner. The Holy Spirit spoke to my heart and soul; my wife spoke to my thought process and helped me implement a practice into our conversations. She said, "The whole time we are talking, I'm praying, 'Lord, lead me in what to say.'"

Taking that line of thought try this when you are in those moments: "Lord, you know her heart and how she's feeling. Give me wisdom and the words to say. In essence, Proverbs 3:5 (AMP) urges us to trust in the Lord with all of our heart, [taking every precaution to] lean not on our own understanding. Then it says, in all of our ways acknowledge him and he will direct our path. It will take some work to break the entrenched cycle of conversation but the result is more understanding.

Love without Control

Control has many moving parts and can take on subtle and the not-so-subtle forms of criticism, lack of support, or inability to focus on the emotional needs of your partner, to more egregious offenses of abuse in all types (physical, mental, emotional, spiritual, etc.). If you ask any man, most feel that they are not controlling, but each of us have a desire to be in control. It is inherent in our human nature, and each person struggles with it in some form. The love Christ died for was freeing, not controlling. God did not create us to be preprogrammed automatons; He gave us free will to choose life with Him or life without Him. Love, where your spouse has true freedom, is when your spouse has freedom of choice without fear of condemnation. The First Epistle of John(4:18, NKJV) makes it clear that "there is no fear in love; but perfect love casts out fear because fear involves torment." Understanding that none of us is perfect in the way that we can perfect our love through continued and intentional submission. The correct view of freedom in love comes without a fear of shut out, ridicule, rejection, or disapproval. This means that a correct understanding of true abiding love means giving up one's desire to control.

Wives who have autonomy become inspired to serve the family unit through leadership, loyalty, and respect. Who wouldn't want that for his wife and their family? Do you want to know why the most successful marriages do not present as a marriage but a close friendship or a relationship where neither could exist without each other? It's because neither person is trying to control the other. When we lay aside our preconceived expectations of a wife or, women, we can begin to encourage our wives' skills and purpose on the earth. Many marriages are dying because the wife is decaying, full of purpose without an avenue to release it.

Proverbs 14:30 (KJV) says, "A heart at peace gives life to the body, but envy rots the bones (KJV)." You read that right. A heart devoid of peace is being limited (controlled by something) and is a breeding ground for envy, hatred, and contempt. We want our wives to be at peace with their place of value to our families. If you are not the best at following the meticulous protocols of balancing checkbooks, paying bills on time, or following tedious IKEA instructions, let her do it! It does not detract from your manhood. You can apply your skills elsewhere. Cook dinner throughout the week, clean up around the house, even fold the laundry, yes you can do all of those things. There is no task too big or too small. Realize that by leaping off your high horse into authentic leadership through a partnership with God, you reap freedom and peace.

The freedom we experience in Christ, the freedom He died for, is so incredible that we should want to lead others to this amazing experience. We feel inspired to be at His side even more, not only because of the gift of salvation He gave us. We reverence Him because He was personally involved in our redemption. We must realize that because God doesn't control us, we need to be free from the desire to control in our lives. Our true freedom enables us to treat our spouse with the same grace God gives us!

Love Wrapped in Grace

Above all things have fervent love for one another, for love will cover a multitude of sins.

— *1 Peter 4:8 (KJV)*

Few people know that love comes with a fine print. Many skip it, and that has led to more disgruntled marriages than we can statistically examine. Real love takes into account that we will fall short of God's love because we're human but it is also balanced with restorative grace.

At the altar during my wedding to my wife, the minister said something that seemed random, "I just want to tell you that love covers a multitude of sins," and while my wife and I chuckled about it, later I understood why he said it. Marriage is an honorable covenant. It is precious, but to err is human. When we do mess up, we have to understand that our "perfect" spouse will not always behave that way; neither will we. We need to be ready to give her the same wide berth of grace we expect when we fall short. It is equally as imperative that we exercise our ability to forgive quickly and ask for forgiveness just as quick.

If you say you love your wife, but harbor painful emotions of resentment, jealousy, or unforgiveness in your heart, you are in dangerous territory. Pride, control, and selfishness are elements of sin lying at the door. You are setting a precedent for more oppressive behaviors within the marriage.

James 5:16 (AMP) says, "Therefore, confess your sins to one another [your false steps, your offenses], and pray for one another, that you may be healed *and* restored. The heartfelt *and* persistent prayer of a righteous man (believer) can accomplish much [when put into action and made effective by God—it is dynamic and can have tremendous power]." Confession creates space for immediate healing. For those attempting to distance themselves from this necessary healing, believe me when I say that you love at your best once you heal, first individually and then together.

The second part in confession is recognizing where your words land. If your wife's mood has changed, what you said landed and you would do well to find out the impact it made. Thirdly, prayer is the part of this equation that is usually missing from this process. Most often, prayers are the last words anyone wants to utter when embroiled in a disagreement. However, when I prayed during arguments, it changed the trajectory of the conversation. How? The invocation of prayer is not a stall tactic; it is a return to the altar for more grace to give and receive what neither of you deserve. It is the ability to be loved during one of your more unlovable moments. That's all that grace is! It is receiving the love that Christ died to give when we were most unlovable. At that moment, your heart can receive healing and power.

This power in turn gives us power for a purpose and the ability to love her more and better. The direct result of heartfelt prayer and an open heart is that you now have the power to forgive, to understand, and, most importantly, to see beyond the offense.

Love, Even in Disagreement

Be angry, and do not sin: do not let the sun go down on your wrath, nor give place to the devil.
—Ephesians 4:25-27 (KJV)."

Have you learned that it's healthy to disagree even in marriage? In fact, disagreement is one way to identify opportunities for you to become more unified. Please understand, unity does not mean carbon copy, rather, it means being likeminded through the process and arriving at the same destination. The scripture says, "How can two walk together except they agree (Amos 3:3, KJV)?" Too often, people conflate disagreements and arguments. While both are uncomfortable, the process and outcomes could not be further apart. Disagreements revolve around the ideas of not finding consensus about a process or its conclusion. Arguments focus on perceptual evidence to prove your own rightness and disprove the other's. Once the emotions get involved and tempers flare and you are off to the races. I know firsthand how difficult it can be to converse without anger controlling you and your words. Let me encourage you that it is possible! Furthermore, you can disagree without removing yourself from the emotional reach of the other person or cause them to withdraw from you. Disagreements are the uncomfortable part of the unification.

They can make you feel like you are growing apart, even if that is not necessarily happening. If that is the case, you might feel immobilized and demoralized as a couple. Movement takes place when individual wills come subject to the unified will.

Because we are human and we do not marry ourselves, there are moments where the wills of both parties in a marriage will not line up exactly. The New Testament shows a moment of deep anguish in Jesus, and yet, we see the sacrifice of His human, individual will for the will of the Father. With many marriages beginning without a strong relationship with the Father, often instead of a surrendering of wills, our wills battle against each other. This battle rages into conversations and even pushes spouses to look for commonality, solace, and security in someone or something else.

If we can reframe a disagreement from this moment forward as a discipline, then it would not hurt quite as much. The discipline I'm referring to isn't punishment but relearning the prescribed conduct for kingdom citizens. There are several truths about discipline that we need to pay attention to if we want even our disagreements to evolve: it can be miserable in the moment, it's painful, it makes you question whether or not the relationship is worth going through this, it produces a greater focus and understanding (Hebrews 12:11, AMP). We are being pruned to become more Christ-like and Christ-looking. God can use our conflicts for moments of discipline. Our spouses serve, as mirrors to our heart postures. You should not get mad if the mirror reflects something that you do not want to see. In one of my favorite movies, *Remember the Titans* Julius tells his teammate and captain Bertier, "Attitude reflects leadership, captain." Man up and behold, take the moment of discipline and grow.

Think back to your biggest fight or longest-lasting disagreement in your marriage. Did that feel like your idea of fellowship? Did your partner walk away, confident in the love you have for her? Did you feel like they knew you or understood you better? As stated, every disagreement reveals an area that you can grow in and before you look to your partner as the root cause, do some self-reflection.

CHAPTER 3

Husbands Love Your Wives

All men have fears, but the brave put down their fears and go forward, sometimes to death, but always to victory.

—Dale Carnegie, *How to Win Friends and Influence People*

Let's talk about your wife: the best thing this side of heaven, your "snookums." Regardless of how you refer to her or how you feel about her in this moment, she is you! Scripture tells us how to treat our wives; we are to treat them *as* we treat ourselves (Ephesians 5:28-29, KJV).

The differences of roles and abilities God gives men and women does not give husbands the right to exercise control over our wives and call it "the natural order of God." If you want a brief history of "toxic masculinity", you can begin there. Treating your wife as yourself is impossible when you regard her as less than, maybe not in word but certainly in deed. When you think of something that you value, the way you behave towards it sets the standard for how others will treat it. For example, in my car and in other cars I will not put my feet on the dashboard while riding in the front passenger's seat. I've seen others do it but it doesn't fly with me. I demand that others, who may be looking for a greater sense of comfort, respect my rules in my car. Similarly, I set the standard for how I want people to treat my body because I own this body. If someone were to walk up to me and touch me inappropriately, I would react in accordance to the violation.

While a husband does not own his wife, neither does a wife own her husband in the human capital sense; respecting your spouse and their freedoms is a two-way street. In First Corinthians 7:4 (KJV) it states, "The wife does not have authority over her own body but yields it to her husband. In the same way, the husband does not have authority over his own body but yields it to his wife." The word authority should start to stick out more now. In the original text, we understand authority as a sort of authorized power, which is why the word 'yield' is there.

When you married your wife, you gave consent to submit unilateral control over your power and will. Thus you allow your partner to have access to and influence in your decisions, actions, and thoughts. For some the real battle is often the battle for your individualism, and more often than not, your selfishness.

No one in his or her right mind would sign up to be or feel owned, right? No one wants to think that the desires of another control them. The beautiful thing is, we belong to our wives and our wives belong to us! We are owned/owners, served/servants, and submitted leaders. First Peter 3:7 (KJV) says, "husbands live with your wives in an understanding way according to knowledge...show her honor and respect as a fellow heir of the grace of life, so that your prayers will not be hindered or ineffective." In those days, a statement like this was considered as radical an idea as it is today. We cannot say enough about how glaring a warning Peter gives. A failure to live with your wife in understanding, knowledge and honor, restricts and renders your prayers ineffective.

During the "Bible days," a husband serving his wife and treating her with respect was almost as heinous as blasphemy. If you want your wife to respect you, then you need to love her and respect her first! Attitude reflects leadership as we all know, but it also lays the house's foundation.

A young married couple, inspiration to my wife and I, did something so beautiful to strengthen their marriage. They created distance between themselves and others while they were learning marriage. The wife remarked that she took her vows very seriously and wanted to learn about the man she vowed to forsake all others for. Her words hit me like a ton of bricks. For all they knew about each other in their dating life, they wanted to go deeper. Deeper didn't mean more facts and dark secrets however, it meant learning how to treat her with a greater level of respect, honor, and ultimately submission of themselves to the unity of marriage.

My wife and I were on the opposite end of the spectrum. We were zealous out of the gate. We wanted to change lives, teach singles, encourage young married people, etc. We had the zeal, but we didn't prioritize learning about each other first. Our marriage counselors were right in saying we should have taken that time. Consequently, not following their advice, we often stumbled into unnecessary misunderstandings early and often. We were the picture-perfect couple in the grocery store, at church services, and any other public place, but when we returned home, we might as well have called for a fire truck because things were on the verge of explosion. We did not take the time to know each other as husband and wife deeply and wholly. My friend and I loved our wives and our married lives; how we learned unity and submission differed greatly. When the scriptures say, "Husbands love your wives...," they were not talking about sex. They also did not prioritize having "me time" above doing activities together. It says clearly to love.

Love Her in Prayer

What does it mean to love your wife? For the moment, let's focus on the spiritual and ask, "Do you love your wife enough to pray for her?" Even in those moments where your feelings were hurt or she got under your skin can you put that aside to bring your concerns to the altar? Prayer is a powerfully underutilized tool in the arsenal of a married man. There is not one scripture in the New Testament that explicitly encourages a husband to pray for his wife. The mandate comes from the example of Christ throughout his life and where he stands now before God interceding for us (Romans 8:34, KJV). When we think about loving something, we do not want any hurt, harm, or danger to come to it. We want that object to always be regarded as important and special and we want to continue to enjoy it at its fullest capacity. When we love someone, we wish for even greater protection. I don't love my car, my job, or my money to the level I love my wife. For that reason, I pray that no hurt, harm, or danger comes to her. We should do the same and when we do; pray that she always knows how important she is to God and you. Pray that she continues to walk and find joy in the journey that you are on with Jesus in marriage. As we pray for our spouses, we can take any emotion and release them to God. As we are in covenant with Him, He does his part to send a response and it's our job to listen and execute. We can't blame God for the answers we choose not to listen to and implement. If God is leading you to devotional time with your wife, there is a reason for it. You may not be wavering but perhaps she is. If God is leading you to get counseling for your deep-seated lust issues it could be because He knows it is beginning to leak into your marriage. When you pray for God to "work on your wife" don't be surprised if the scalpel turns your way. In your union, a prayer for your spouse *is* a prayer for yourself, because God has no interest in taking sides. His interest is in producing the fruit!

Love Her With Your Eyes

When we feed ourselves a cuisine of preference and fantasy, we willingly deny anything that does not satisfy our palate; that is also true in marriage. That idea may seem shallow to some, but would you have married your wife if you were not physically attracted to her? Likely not. Additionally, her glowing personality and willingness to put up with you, keep you locked in. Unfortunately, while we grow in love, we also grow older, and things that were once high might sag; tight things tend to stretch and hang. Such is life.

It isn't a secret that men are visual creatures. Therefore, without command or request, our appetite sends messages to our eyes to «feed me." Our eyes start to roam, looking for those pre-covenant preferences. Is it wrong to have had preferences? Of course not. It is natural to desire to look at what you enjoyed looking at before you took your vows. But, the question is, how are you looking at your former preferences and why? Have you surrendered looking at individuals who fit that preference with lust leaving only genuine, brief, appreciation? Be honest and ask God to help you to develop strategies for how to abolish lustful desires from your eyes and mind.

Job said he had to make a covenant with his eyes not to look upon a woman with lust, because he was married (Job 31:1, KJV). Jonathan Welton, author of *Eyes of Honor: Training for Purity and Righteousness*, made this poignant statement about this:

> Most men are still trying to fight temptation the same way that Job did. I am not giving license for looking lustfully, but I do need to state that 'don't' is never going to be a successful strategy. There is a fundamental flaw in this type of

approach. Imagine if I were to create a law stating that it is a sin to think of oranges. The obvious directive: "Don't think of oranges." Instead of helping you to avoid sin, the law immediately stirs within you the desire to rebel.

I love a good juicy orange, especially clementine. Well, I guess that makes me a sinner. Jonathan makes a powerful illustration that the war in our members (Romans 8, KJV) is real! A beautiful image in front of you can leave any of us deprioritizing the ring on our finger or the covenant in our heart. Therefore, the issue is appreciating beauty like you would a beautiful landscape or seeing your favorite sport played at the highest level. Appreciation like this won't make you want to go after something in the heat of passion.

When I asked my dad about how to appreciate beauty without being lustful, he said, "God made beauty all around us. If I can't take in the beauty without desiring [to sexually have] it, the problem isn't with the beauty, it's me and with what I want to do with it." He couldn't have been more right and it may be painful to see yourself as the problem. For too long we have placed the onus on women to alter their behaviors so that men do not fall, no longer. We should wage war on the unruly parts of ourselves so that we do not expect others to do it for us. When you fail to do this, you unintentionally invite fantasy to plague your thought life and lead you to compromised footing; a fall is close by.

When you start to fantasize, you may have to resort to justifying your fantasies which are ultimately a vain attempt to cover your imagined infidelity. God forbid an opportunity to act on the fantasy presents itself. The thought now has good soil to germinate and grow that seed of infidelity. You are in danger of setting your feet on the path of lust. I cannot speak for you, but I have sinned with my eyes. As such, I have committed adultery in my heart. I openly repent because I do not want any part of a lustful, deceitful, covenant-breaking heart. Are you with me? The thing is, your behavior didn't start moments before you met your wife and the valve is not easily turned off afterwards. Why then do we continue to toggle with the valve?

How do we get control of this area of our lives? Our eyes must be focused. Like Job, we have to put boundaries on what we are willingly looking at. Are your eyes focused only on your wife, and are your feet headed in the same direction? Meaning, do you value her more than you value the next nice-looking woman who walks by or shows you attention? Here is the kicker: when you start to let your eyes slip and leave your heart unguarded against lustful thoughts, you may not even end up with someone as attractive or loving as your wife! You could end up with someone who is willing to stroke your ego and keep your entertained. The Enemy is not obligated to pair you with your number-one preference. He just has to get you close enough to what you would tolerate!

Pornography

I felt it necessary to address this issue head on because in many religious circles the conversation about pornographic addiction is just now getting the attention it so desperately deserves. In the past, this conversation focuses on sin or lust and ends with a wagging finger and deep-seated shame. It doesn't have to be that way anymore. Today, you can choose to be part of healthy conversations that look to normalize stages of life, hold you to the standard of your salvation, and equip you with tools to win the battle over your mind, your eyes, and your appetite.

As someone who previously battled with this (hidden) issue, I am now living in freedom. I can tell you firsthand that whether you were an infrequent participant or a binge-watcher, your marriage will have to deal with this issue. You likely have dealt with it for a long time on your own and now that you are married, you may look to continue this battle by yourself. You cannot win that way and you will hurt your wife emotionally, mentally, and spiritually if you continue to hide it. Pornography is a real issue that I wish would have never harmed your childhood, sexual development, or relationships. You may say, "It's not a big deal," but that is the great deception. When you think about how long you've had a relationship with pornography and masturbation, it may be longer than your years of formal education. That makes this topic a big deal!

Pornography places you in the middle of your lust and tells you to enjoy the beauty, the activity, the release, but the memories of the images are burned into your retinas. Pornography is not the same as watching an episode of *The Office*, *Property Brothers*, or the plethora of *CSI* shows. The images that you see pique your interest and activate your brain's pleasure center. The bio-chemical, dopamine, that is released in the process from arousal to orgasm records the process, holds the methods, and makes you want to go back for more. Pornography is not just a bad habit, it's a chemically induced high, which makes it even harder to break; quitting cold turkey, for many, is nearly impossible.

Even in your marriage, if you have struggled with pornography at any level, you have to deal with this by: repenting, finding an accountability partner, connecting to a community of men who are actively pursuing freedom, identifying what your triggers are, and placing boundaries around them. For some, counseling may be necessary.

Jesus said if you look at a woman with lust in your heart, it's as if you've already done the deed (Matthew 5:27-28). That is not a license to follow through with an affair. Some might think, "Well, if I've already been guilty of it, I might as well enjoy the way down."

There is a stark difference between the look and the action. However, the damage to the heart is done. You do not have to stay a slave to this cycle. Christ came to set you free and with him no addiction or habitual sin can hold you! If you take the time now to earnestly repent there is no question that you can be made new even in your mind! Let Christ take that struggle and give you victory! "If any man be in Christ, he is a new creature: old things are passed away; behold all things are become new (2 Corinthians 5:17, KJV).

Honor Begins in the Thoughts

Part of Christ's ministry was moving beyond the outward piety of that time to inward reformation. His disciples saw this, writing that we should meditate or think on things that are lovely, pure, commendable, and admirable (Philippians 4:8, KJV). Your covenant marriage in God's eyes is lovely, pure, commendable, and admirable. It is good to meditate on how to pursue living out that marriage with God as the center. At the same time, we must endeavor to avoid falling into making an idol of your marriage but holding this relationship in higher esteem than other relationships; that is honor. Honor does not begin in your actions; it begins in the mind, as does dishonor. If your thoughts are dishonorable, your actions toward your wife will be dishonorable.

Remember that couple who inspired my wife and me? He has built a high level of honor toward his wife. For example, he said "When I'm on business trips, I literally act like she is in the bathroom when I am out to eat, so when I am approached or hit on, in my mind she's on her way back to the table." While this may seem extreme to some, he took a clear stance on how he would honor his wife in her presence and in her absence. That level of purposeful choosing exemplifies how you love and honor your wife in your mind.

If we go one-step deeper, when you are upset with her and you go into another room to cool off, what you say about her in your head matters. If you thought dishonor was only when you spoke to people outside of your marriage, you missed it. The thoughts in your head show in the way you're being dishonorable toward her. Proverbs 23:7 (KJV) says, "As a man thinketh in his heart so is he" there is no question that if you dishonor your wife in your thoughts you will eventually dishonor her.

I have been so upset with my wife that I had to choose to sit quietly while actively steering my thoughts away from dishonor. Rather than belittling her or going so far as to assassinate her character in my mind, I choose to think about the problem objectively, not subjectively. Meaning I attack the problem and not my wife, even in my mind; the battle starts with how you view her. This can be a difficult task because the muscle of honor is not one we use often enough. Too often we feel justified when comments are seemingly aimed at attacking our character or directed towards our "manhood." How you respond to those moments reveal your mental capacity to love her, contrasted against, your profession "to always love and to cherish" her. The issue is not whether you love her but in what spaces you love her.

A culture of honor makes the consistent choice to think, regard, esteem, and uphold your wife highly. Being married in the mind is a challenge because we live under the illusion that we can be married in a covenant, married in the bedroom, and yet single in our mind. The Apostle James would qualify that as double-minded (James 1:8, KJV) and would identify instability in everything that you do. I am so confident that if you have fallen to double mindedness God can show you where you lowered your guard and help you reinforce your gates with his word before causing irreparable harm to your marriage.

Your heart, mind and soul needs the renewing and transformative power of God. Then and only then can you see your wife as an equal image bearer of Christ, worthy of honor as a member of the body.

Love Her with Your Hands

How to love your wife sexually—this is the part so many of you have been waiting on. Men enjoy sex and appreciate it in a variety of ways. Some like it this way and others that way, but the ultimate goal for most is pleasure. That pleasure was highly fantasized at an early age and our introduction to sex varies from person to person. Some learned about love in a romantic sense, others in horrific and premature ways that left scars. Regardless of however you came to know about sex and intimacy, we all have some unlearning to do.

While the Bible teaches that men should remain celibate until their wedding day that may not be possible. So, we approach the conversation of sex and intimacy by first dismantling fantasy and shadows of relationships past to firmly grasp reality. The woman you married is a real person. The woman you pledged your life to is a real person who is yours to have, hold, and cherish with your hands. Those images of your past, in your mind, or on that screen are just that. Holding on to them is like trying to hold on to steam.

In the beginning, we see God involved in every detail of creation. As a carpenter, Christ was intimately involved with hands-on projects. As Savior, he was intimately invested in the lives he touched. To be clear, I am not insinuating that Christ was sexually involved with those he touched. All touch is not sexual, but touch, has a way of bringing us into connection with another person. Whether that connection makes mountains of confidence or valleys of despair is based on how the touch is perceived and by whom it is performed. Jesus performed miracles, not just by using his words, but also by the extension of his hands. His ministry approach never left the church feeling threatened, abused, powerless, or manipulated. He knew their history and how best to love them.

While you may know your wife's sexual and relationship history, marriage invites you to explore her more intimately. You will need to be keenly aware of how you approach her because your past experiences have ways of creeping in. They may appear as innocent preferences until you find the root, where more telling story of trauma lies.

Whether married, engaged, or single, we all have needed or still need to heal from our traumatic memories. Those memories may be the root cause for fantasies. You may be wondering, "Can't I fantasize about my wife?" I encourage you to do so only if you can make certain that what inspired the fantasy was not influenced by images in the media or from coveting another man's wife. Fantasy; an exercise of the mind's creativity, can be easily corrupted and manipulated if you do not have safeguards in place to fight thoughts of immoral thoughts and fantasies. These have damaging effects on the intimacy we desire to have with our wives because we conceal fantasy. I'd hazard a guess that if our fantasy lives were put into print or acted out on screen, the divorce rate would double. God is the progenitor of creativity and can inspire you without needing to expose you to ideas detrimental to your peace. We have to ensure that we only use fantasy in creative ways to honor and pleasure our wives. Creativity, as a road map, invites her to be seen and valued because she is included in the process. When we use fantasy as a road map, it ends in frustration because it's performative. At best, you are an actor going through the motions and at worst it leaves your wife feeling rejected or devalued. Believe me when I say that she can see the reel playing in your eyes. She has to be enough; she has to be the object of your desire.

When Christ loved the church, he wasn't acting out what he saw other would-be-saviors doing. He certainly did not spend his time wondering what it would be like if he chose any other people to enter into a covenant with. He was willing to take the challenging journey of loving her intimately; just her. The challenge of loving her with your hands is exploratory in nature. Sex for the sake of sex does not mean you know your wife intimately. As sex isn't just about passion but connection, your exploration must be a combination of meaningful conversation and speaking her love language. Conversation sustains connection; speaking her love language satisfies her need to feel valued and understood. When the combination of these is right, she has the capacity to meet or exceed your desires and will be more willing to let you explore her more intimately. Sexual exploration is a part of marriage that you should spend a lifetime learning.

During college, someone asked me what I thought marriage would be like, and my response was "A life spent learning my wife's mind, body, and spirit." Then came the wedding night. I thought I was gearing up to put it down. After all, I was a virgin with hours of experience in fantasy, a master's degree in self-pleasure, and I had logged over two thousand volunteer hours of pornography in my 20+ years; I should have known what I was doing, right? Needless to say, my wife laughed at me. How demoralizing! I mean, I thought I was laying it down, but she said it was clear I was trying to act out what I saw. What she was really saying was that I was not interested in learning me, but in fulfilling my fantasies on her body.

How many marriages have been destroyed because intimacy is performative and not intimately educational? How does your wife respond when you say this, kiss there, or touch her in a certain way without request? Do you know where most of her tension resides and do you work to relieve it or do you speed to your climax while neglecting hers?

"Well, what do I do when I am not sexually attracted to my wife anymore?" Before answering, examine what your appetite has been. The images that have your attention could be affecting your ability to see your wife as attractive by reason of comparison. Pairing that with growing discontentment which is lending itself to contempt and you have a ticking time bomb on your hands. Before you place the blame on what she is not doing, especially for your eyes, examine what has changed in you since she was the most beautiful woman in your world. The burden of proof isn't on her to show how she hasn't maintained her picture-perfect self. Instead, it is on you because as you move closer to images and interest outside of the covenant, it causes you to be colder to what used to be a deeply passionate marriage. That means you have to be honest and transparent about what is going on in your head. How we see our wives does affect how we perform in the bedroom and what messages she receives during intercourse.

Love Her with Your Soul

Today, because of the prevalence of dating apps and websites, we often look out for one terrible word that all of them use: *compatibility*. Compatibility is defined as two things that can exist together without conflict or problem; to get along with something else. It can be a misleading metric in a relationship, because while two attributes or characteristics seem to play well together, the differing levels of intensity in a marriage can interact in beautiful or dangerous ways. For example, a couple who may be highly intellectual, which makes for great conversation when they talk about politics, academic literature and logic. But when they take that intellectual approach to subjects like who should apologize first or who forgot to close the refrigerator, things can get ugly pretty quickly. Facts, timelines, statistics and others start flying and truth is lost in the fray. Dating makes compatibility seem like the desired end for any successful relationship. In fact, we mistakenly looked for the areas in which we were exactly the same to determine whether or not to continue pursuing the relationship. While compatibility gets you in the door, it cannot sustain a relationship at the level we desire to be connected. To begin loving like Christ beyond common interests or characteristics, we have to look at what keeps our hearts singularly focused on one mate.

The Book of Hosea tells the story of a prophet instructed to marry a prostitute and love her as a wife. Now, pause right here. I am not comparing your wife to his wife in any way. The

story points to the fact that societally, she was a liability; emotionally, she was a liability; mentally, she was a liability, too, because he would spend the lion's share of his time trying to prove to her that beyond all of that, she was his choice. Hosea points to the fact that she had nothing to offer at the present even though her being a prostitute did not render her unlovable. She may have been in a profession that she would never have chosen if given the chance; she was still worthy of love. Hosea, in this sense, is a foreshadowing of the condition Christ saw his bride.

In the Ten Commandments God instructs us to love God with all of our soul without asking if we have anything in common or if we had anything to barter. It is saying, ``If we strip away all of the blessings, favors, possessions, the feel-good moments, and the mistakes, do you love me?" Similarly, your wife wants to know the answer to this question, sometimes often and other times unsolicited. She wants to know if beyond her looks, the intimate physical experiences you have shared, and beyond the fact that she has done so much for you, if she is enough to be your one and only.

I imagine my own wife with tears in her eyes asking this and it breaks my heart to think she should ever have to. When you love your wife with your soul, you love her in the choices you make, your day-dreams, your speech, your thoughtfulness, and your presence. Like Hosea and Christ, we should love our wives no matter the seasons she goes through. We need to love her in her moments of triumph and the ones she never wants to have repeated. When we entered into this covenant, we took a vow that we would love her "for richer or for poorer, in sickness and in health, to love and to cherish," we vowed to love her soulfully. Men; as we love God with all that we are, the secondary consequence is that our wives should feel the radiance of that love without question.

CHAPTER 4

As Christ

A selfless man will be characterized by patience, restraint, and an eagerness to do what is best for the object of his affections.

—*What He Must Be: ...If He Wants to Marry My Daughter*, Voddie Baucham Jr.

MANY BELIEVERS TODAY WOULD AGREE that Christ is the model for how we can live lives that honor God and impact society and culture. As He is our example, He is our answer to every problem. While that sounds like good news, we men have an overreliance on our abilities both intellectually and physically. If we can't do it with our heads we try to achieve and accomplish tasks with our hands. In either situation we are trying to produce something of ourselves. That means that we can only be the answer to the things that are temporal not things that are eternal

Dr. Matthew Stevenson III says, "Whenever God wants to do something on Earth or desires to change a person, he sends a person." Heaven's response to the issue of sin was resolved in the life of the God King Jesus. Heaven's response to the issues of failed covenant, seen in the Old Testament, is resolved in Christ and offered to each of us through relationship. When Christ called us into covenant with him, He became Savior and husband to the church.

I grew up with a father who was phenomenal in many ways. While I observed him to be an exemplary husband, I was an on-looker. It was my mother who had firsthand knowledge of how he was as a husband. Their private conversations and memories were all secondhand knowledge to me.

If we look at my father as an example of how to be a husband, we may see ebbs and flows of similarities between him and Christ. And for those of you reading who already go above and beyond for your mate (kudos to you!) will find nothing to help you grow further in Christ. But when we measure ourselves against the greatest example of a husband who has made every provision for His bride, and awaits her with patience, we see that some areas that we—or perhaps society value start to look more like participation trophies.

I want to look at Isaiah 43:4 (KJV) to build on this premise. It is easy to overlook, but it is very important: "Since you are cherished and precious in my eyes, and because I love you dearly and want to honor you, I willingly give up nations in exchange for you—a man to save your life."

Did you see that? He called His people cherished! Precious! Not in a deranged way like Gollum and his Precious from *The Lord of the Rings* or *the Hobbit*, but with genuine affection, as though we are jewels of unmatched value. Jesus came "to seek and to save the lost (Luke, 19:10, NIV). Why did He come for the lost? He showed that you aren't be a good husband until you set your heart on a crash course of reclamation.

God's plan for Jesus and His bride has always been one of re-demption. Think of this: if Christ had not come, there would be no relief from sin, despair, hurt, loneliness, rejection, depression, igno-rance, sickness and so much more. These are unfortunately part of the human condition as a result of the fall God knew that a solution had to come in the form of his original intention for us, which was everlasting union. You may not be Jesus but you can certainly bring relief through your submission.

As men, we often attempt to play the part of the hero and feeling as if we rescued our wife in some way. You may have felt you rescued her from a number of things but I caution you not to think so highly because you too needed the Savior. Being her hero is not your burden to bear. We feel burdened to be her savior through an unfounded "superhero complex" until we can no longer say strong for her or ourselves. Falling short triggers despair because despite all of your efforts, she's still hurting. When this happens it's easy to feel as though you're "not enough." One warning for many would-be heroes is that in your quest for the perfect marriage and wife, anything you do that falls short of perfection can lead you to despair. Deep-rooted despair is responsible for many insecurities in a marriage.

In order to understand how to love your wife well, you have to look at the person of Jesus Christ, who from heaven's perspective is the husband coming to receive his wife. First, we examine him as the perfect, whole husband, and while this is by no means an exhaustive analysis of Christ, in Him we find three qualities of marriage to examine: identity, character, and a look into His movements.

Identity

Christ was firmly planted in who He was and that came after His baptism when His Father spoke His identity over Him. Interestingly enough, while He never forgot His identity, the world ran Him through the gamut of identities. They said things such as, "Is not this the carpenter's son?" They questioned His influence: "Can any good thing come out of Nazareth?" They questioned His lineage in an attempt to make His background common and His identity to be just like any other carpenter's son. God had already given Jesus His identity and the most dangerous thing about a kingdom minded husband is one who knows his identity. While being fully aware of his family's history and can empathize with their struggles he remains unshakeable. It's true Jesus came through a lineage of humans. More specifically in his family were idol worshippers, murders, liars, priests, cheaters, insecure people, kings, and one supposedly infamous harlot. Had He taken His identity from His family history, he would have aborted the identity God sent Him with: His son and the espoused husbandman of the church!

Some men marry hoping to discover an identity they never received from their father. This results in them only being able to love by providing for their family, because the only identity they saw modeled was that of a provider—not a lover, friend or worshipper. When Jesus received the words from the Father during His baptism, He stepped into the fullness of His identity. He says later in the Gospel of John, "I can only do what I have seen the Father do (John 5:19, KJV)."

If you were to ask yourself of the example you saw or didn't see of your father as a husband, rather than just a father, would you see one of compassion, humility, sacrifice, or providing security for his wife? The painful realization is that sometimes we don't see examples of these, and so we begin marriage with a polarized view of it. Either we become the failed husband or we become the superhero husband. The first is rooted in selfishness while the second is rooted in performance. However, neither are indications of stability in relationship with God. Jesus showed through the example of His life that the most exemplary husbands are submitted sons who know who they are.

Character

Your character which has been shaped by years of experience is somewhat fixed in many of your minds. Where we have to challenge ourselves is to reject the idea that we have arrived at our final destination. Marriages die when either spouse, but in this case husbands, feel like they only need to change when stability is threatened. Relationships evolve and mature over time and so character should also mature. Jesus was the example of mature character and the measuring stick of what we should strive for.

What was Jesus like while he walked the Earth? We have some evidence that points to his righteous anger, care in navigating sensitive topics in people's lives, and confidence. Many were taught in Sunday school that God is love. Since God is love (1 John 4:16, KJV) and Jesus is the Son of God being fully God and fully man, Jesus' character must be that of the Father. So, the answer was in front of us the entire time and we constantly miss it. 1 Corinthians 13:4-8 is a common passage; we quote this scripture as if it is talking about love only as an attribute. It truly speaks about how Christ, the husband, lived. "Love is patient, love is kind. It does not envy, it does not boast, it is not proud, it does not dishonor others, it is not self-seeking, it is not easily angered, it keeps no record of wrongs. Love does not delight in evil, but it rejoices with the truth. It always protects, always trusts, always hopes, and always perseveres. Love never fails... " If we replace love with Jesus, because they are synonymous, we get a better understanding of what it looks like to be a husband, try it.

Now if you put your name in there does all of that still ring true? Are you patient, are you kind? Do you envy or do you boast? Are you proud? Do you dishonor others, are you self-seeking, are you easily angered, and do you keep a record of wrongs? Do you delight in evil instead of rejoicing in the truth? Do you always protect, always trust, always hope, always preserve? Are you unfailing? The areas in which you find yourself hesitating or outright saying no, are the areas you can pray and ask God to guide you. Even as I write this, I am repenting because, like many of you, I do some of these some of the time, but I want to do all of these all of the time as God empowers me. It is not impossible it is more within your reach than you realize!

Movement

You might be wondering the importance of examining Christ's movements. Primarily because He did not live sedentary life. Even though he was popular in his area, nothing he did was for popularity or attention; he did it out of love. He did not live in front of a worker's bench or in a man cave. Christ was active during his time on Earth. Even at twelve years old, he went missing from his parents but made his way to the synagogue. Years later, he attended a wedding and his mother demanded servants to follow him around to do his bidding. We find him being jostled by a crowd while a woman crawls through them just to get to him because he was in transit. He didn't waste energy or effort because he was intentional.

What have you made up your mind and followed through with? I'm sure you planned a date night or vacation, did you pull the trigger? You planned to bring flowers but that argument before you arrived at the store made you lose momentum. Did the argument disqualify her from deserving levels of your affection? When was the last time you woke up earlier than her to set things in order so that both of your mornings could run smoother? Why is there more intentional energy for things outside of the home? We can be intentional about waking up early for an important meeting or scheduling long overdue time with your boys but not for time with your wife. Comparatively, the first Law of Thermodynamics says that energy isn't created or destroyed it can only be transferred from one form to another. Would you be willing to take the energy you apply outside of your marriage into your marriage?

You may say it does not take all of that when in fact, it does and you know it. In many of the marriages I have worked with, wives miss their husbands' spontaneity and willingness to do the little things to keep them happy. If you remember it was the little things that you did that made her feel special.

My wife has a favorite drink from our local convenience store. For no other reason than to make her happy and let her know, I am paying attention, I stop in to get the drink before going home. "What's this for?" she asked me. "Nothing," I replied. "You haven't had one in a while and I know that you probably craved one." She gushes because it wasn't about the item, it was about the fact that I was intentional about including her. I was thinking about her and I acted upon it. This may not happen often but it should not be so scarce that your last act hangs as a memorial in her memory. In fact, take the time to put it in your phone calendar to 'buy roses for your wife' three weeks from today, they can only be her favorites. And while you are at it, plan date night next month. Do it right now! If you can think of anything else now is the time to add it to your calendar.

Christ stayed in motion, moving TOWARD destiny. While your movement may not seem as grandiose, are you moving your relationship with your wife closer to the reflection of your parents or towards the image God wants for you? Arguments, criticism, withholding sex, selfishness, and infidelity are examples of movements away from the goal. There will always be movement but there are forces at work on a crash course to derail it. The passage says, "we wrestle not against flesh and blood… (Ephesians 6:12, KJV)" I believe this alludes to the fact that you are waging a war of momentum. If you spent more time building and speaking life over one another, you would have more momentum.

The Secret Place

Christ had a secret place where he could be alone, just His Father and Him. In that place he could off load the weight of the journey and the expectations of those who walked with Him. There He talked to God about the pain of being misunderstood and the line between his divinity and his humanity. In that place, Christ didn't have to be anything for anyone, he could be himself and commune with his Father. His friends couldn't pump him up there and his followers couldn't pull on his anointing. In this area, we have to carve out a place, a space, a time to be ourselves. The quiet, prayerful place is freeing. There, you can place the weight of expectation and the shortcomings we often encounter. The secret place may not look like anyone else's but it's yours. It may be your car ride on the way to work, a path you take to get away or moments at night when everyone is asleep. Wherever your secret place is, prioritize your time there even if it's just ten minutes to have a brief huddle with God. The length of time is not as important as the heart posture, but certainly endeavor to spend time here.

In prayer and meditation, you can receive necessary peace and strength to continue another day. We must start by shedding our preconceived notions and conclusions about whatever is burdening us, accepting the will and way of God through repentance and turning to Him wholly. Until we are ready to "Times of refreshing come from the present of the Lord Acts 3:19 (KJV)". Christ placed great value on prayer and we should do the same.

Your prayer might look something like this:

Father, I am thankful that I have the time with you. I acknowledge that you are the head of my life and God of my heart. I repent for believing that I can lead my wife without your wisdom. All that I am and have is because of your grace and mercy. Please speak to my heart, fill me with your wisdom and lead me as I lead my marriage in covenant with you. Grant me strength to keep going, hope to keep believing and love for my wife so that she sees all of you in me!

Christ the Whole Husband

Before continuing, it would be unwise to ignore the fact that a good husband is a healed husband. If you are to be like Christ in your marriage, you cannot look at Christ without the cross. You have to understand that in his death and burial he was preparing to rise as a 'whole' husband. Therefore, you might hear some speak about the necessity to be 'whole' husband and there is truth to that. When Christ got up from his grave, he challenged his disciples to put their fingers in the wounds. He does not wince, he does not smack their hand away, he does not even call them out of their names. What amazing self-control right? No, he was healed but his wounds did not disappear so in a sense, he was not "whole" as we understand wholeness. The wounded area might still be there, the narrative of the past may even come up in conversation but if it still stings, guess what, you need more healing! Whether those areas are serial disappointments, destructive tempers, unresolved romantic or parental relationships, a hypersensitive fight-or-flight mechanism, traumatic experiences, etc. they all can make for thorny soil areas.

How have you gone after your healing? Have you masked your recovery so everyone thinks you are doing well while simultaneously barely feeling like yourself? Do you dwell on failures, hurts, words from those who mishandled you and find yourself going in circles trying to salve the wound? I can assure you whatever has not healed nor fully restored in you before marriage will come out with unintended veracity and consequence. Unresolved areas become thorny ground or a spark for a misunderstanding and a disagreement. The enemy knows too many won't seek deep healing and so attacks will come against your marriage from years that predated the altar. "Courtship is the time for sowing those seeds which will grow up ten years later into domestic hatred," C.S. Lewis, "The Screwtape Letters." Placing a sentry to guard those vulnerable areas prolongs the inability to fully trust and be trusted. In order to understand these areas, you need to have a community of people who are not interested in you romantically but who are invested in you mentally, emotionally, and spiritually. Even then, your circle must be tight so that the reflection is genuine and not a fabricated version of who they want you to become or who they need you to become in order to achieve their own selfish gains.

Jesus asks his disciples "who do they say that I am?" then "who do you say that I am?" He needed to know that they saw him for who he was not what others had put on him to be. You and your friends have a duty to help each other be their best selves but also their most authentic. They are the ones who should point to the fact that you are still bleeding in your testimony, offended in your reflection and angry in your silence and a myriad of other situations.

To conclude this chapter, I offer this prayer for you. This is necessary especially if you have never had your father pronounce identity over you in a positive way, aligning your life with God's will. I ask that God would settle your identity firmly in Him as a good man, free of addiction, a servant-leader, a man of authority and with integrity. You are not the embodiment of past shortcomings, a carbon copy of broken men in your family, nor will you ever be. I pray that you will be wise in the things of God and man, always loving and never wavering or confused about who you are in Christ.

CHAPTER 5

As Christ Loved the Church

We know the depth of someone's love for us in what it costs him, in how little we deserve it, in the greatness of the benefits we receive in being loved and by the freedom with which they love us.

—John Piper, taken from the sermon "The Depth of Christ's Love: It's Cost"

IT IS AN AMAZING THING to witness a love story unfold before your eyes. To see the spark in two lovers when they speak about each other and that sometimes quaint and other times deliberate smile that takes over the lower half of their faces. The palpable annoyance on the face of outsiders who feel their conversations dominated by reminders of their relationship. The never-ending droning about their characteristics and amazing qualities. No matter the subject, it can always be tied back to their lover. The stages of courtship are as beautiful as they are laborious.

The world is a lot like those on the outside [of said relationship]. It is nauseating to hear people talk about their lover.

Even more infuriating to hear what the lover says about them repeated as if it is an incantation; a recitation for a weird trance. Things like, "I have loved you with an everlasting love" or "I want you to prosper even as your soul prospers" (3 John 2:2, KJV). Our lover wants us to know that we are loved beyond every shadow of doubt. My goodness! What a wonderful lover the church has. Still, the story in the middle is quite tragic. The hero and lover sacrifices his life to reclaim all of her, which is the church. In those few abysmal days following his death, I can imagine a sense of loss, confusion, hopelessness and more. As the story goes, he comes back to life, glorified and just like that, He restored hope! All for her; the church. The story isn't called The Passion simply because he was a loving person. No, he had an objective for his love; the passionate and loving reclamation of the people.

From our perspective, the backstory of the church is bleak and fraught with miscues, identity crises, with flashes of good. In some of our marriages, our backstory is much like the churches. Not everyone has a deep story or some dark past that they are running from. Nevertheless, everyone has insecurities and varying needs that have not been met by parents, pastors, or partners. Specifically, every woman no matter how resilient, proud or otherwise has areas that are calloused, some areas that are infected and others, well, it's just really dusty back there and greater still are the areas 'KEEP OUT'. Yes, that includes you Prince Charming.

Calloused, infected, dusty, off limits. Now before the paragraph continues let's do a self-check. What areas in you meet the criteria? Maybe your Father or mother never said 'I love you' without it being attached to a request or reprimand. Perhaps you have secrets that you have subscribed to the fact that it would end you or your current relationships, whether true or not. You have dreams that aren't dead but no one is pushing you to shake them for revival either. And then, what about that family member, pastor, ex, etc. that comes up in casual conversation that stings just hearing their name. A repressed memory or perhaps just a repetitively painful one. Honesty may be a key but it's not the only one you'll need to blow the walls off your love fortress.

The church in its simplest definition means a group of people who look to follow, trust, and know God through the person of Jesus Christ and capitalize on the opportunity to introduce a loving savior to the world. But the church is full of people in various cycles of their lives. Broken, suffering, at times lost, unfocused in purpose, unsure of identity is what makes up parts of the church. All the while, we find that we are loved beyond explanation. If we remain in this broken space, it is a denial of the sacrifice and an absolute shunning of the gift of an abundant life promised to us through Christ.

The value of a good husband is in his patient, consistent approach to the tough areas of his wife and does not shy away from the challenge. Husbands by nature are problem solvers or at least we think we are. Until we step into identity in Christ, we will stop employing sledgehammers and start getting shovels. Most solutions would meet less resistance if patience didn't run out so quickly. Equally as important, if you go in looking to identify a problem and one does not develop you might look to your spouse as the problem and that she needs the fix.

Christ Served with Joy

When we read the Bible in English, we often fail to benefit from the weight of translated words. For example, there are approximately six words for love in Greek and eleven in Arabic. However, there is only one word for love in English. It would not be too difficult to recognize that because of these transliterations, we also lose the tenor of the text, that is, the sense of meaning. We ascribe certain feelings to the text based on how we would feel in that moment.

When Jesus was in the temple, we know that he was frustrated, but we do not know his feelings when he was in the desert on day twenty-two. We don't know how he felt standing on water, waiting for Peter to walk. The struggle we face while we read is how much of what we are feeling correlates with what the character is feeling.

If I can infer one thing about the God-man, it was that he set the tone for how we should serve. Matthew 20:28 (KJV) is clear that Christ did not come to be served but to serve. However, it never once mentioned that he did it in joy. Theatrically and pictorially, we often see Jesus looking meek or just downright sad. Despite the fact, we reference Hebrews 12:2 (NIV), "for the joy set before him he endured the cross, scorning the shame…" that is not enough to infer that he lived a life of serving with joy. We often infer his emotions through his response to circumstances around him in a given text. Still, it would be unwise to assume the totality of His emotional state in just a few verses.

How did Christ perform miracle after miracle and serve with joy? In today's church, we rarely hear conversations about real joy, at least not to the extent that we should. How to live out the joy Christ promises is seldom taught. We will quote that the "Do not grieve, the joy of the Lord is our strength (Nehemiah 8:10, NIV)," while struggling in our confidence. Though used interchangeably joy and happiness are defined differently. Happiness is many positive emotions and infrequent, but not absent, negative emotions. According to the American Psychological Association, joy is "a feeling of extreme gladness, delight, or exaltation of the spirit arising from a sense of well-being or satisfaction."

In Sunday school, we learned about the Fruit of the Spirit by cutting them out individually and gluing them separately to a sheet of paper. Then we rehearse the Fruit of the Holy Spirit (Galatians 5,

KJV), never understanding that the fruit is housed within a system of love. Operating without one of those fruits is to not to have a full understanding of real love. We cannot discuss being a husband, serving in love, led by the Holy Spirit, and overlook that love is a requirement for joy.

Serving with joy means that you have the right perspective and the right spirit within you. The right perspective is at the end of it all God is going to get glory and victory through it all. The right points to each word, action, or activity point to a true dependence and trust in God. The right perspective and the right spirit settle us. You may not always have the right perspective but the right spirit adjusts the lens. When you do not have the right spirit, you need to be renewed (Psalm 51:10, KJV)! In the garden, Jesus modeled how to do it when he prayed, "thy will be done on earth as it is in heaven (Matthew 6:10, KJV)." The amount of humility needed to put down your will and allow God's will without throwing a tantrum or quitting is not small.

There is a song by Richard Smallwood that my dad's best friend, "Uncle Walt" used to sing. No one could ever sing it like him even to this day. I can still hear him singing it. "Jesus You're the Center of My Joy!" The words continue: "All that's good and perfect comes from you. You're the heart of my contentment, hope for all I do. Jesus, you're the center of my joy." When the Glory of God is the center of your hope, the focal point of your doing, you begin to operate as an unashamed son of God. That means you are satisfied knowing that God has a plan, has all of the power, has a defeated enemy, and has the ultimate victory.

Christ served completely satisfied in his relationship with the Father, knowing that by serving others, he honored God. Looking again we might be able to read Ephesians 5:25 (KJV), husbands serve your wives [with joy] as Christ served the church [with joy]. It doesn't change what the Apostle is implying; instead, we find an equally important focus on love as an act of serving rather than purely an emotion.

So, what does serving with joy look like? Here are five easy principles:

1. Accept- Accept your identity as a son of God. You may be flawed, but you are redeemed and chosen (John 1:12)

2. Address the roadblocks - Talk to God about areas in which it may be hard to serve (Galatians 6:4, AMP)

3. Do It for God - Serve as if God is the recipient of your actions and words (Ephesians 6:7-8, NIV)

4. Trust- Learning to trust God with the outcomes and having peace with His will (Proverbs 3:3-5, KJV)

Joy is not a fleeting emotion. It is a climate that must be cultivated and maintained. Likely, you have not built an appetite for joy. If you had, you would be firmer in your faith, more content in the plans of God and satisfied in your growing relationship with him. Instead, we have no strength through tough moments. We question God even in areas that we have seen the miraculous occur, and we have frequent identity crises that get "resolved" through more work. You cannot serve with joy in that headspace.

Have you disciplined your emotions and soul to remain in joy when serving your wife? Previously, you may not have had a picture of what that looks like. Men if you want to grow in connection to your wife, and ultimately connected to the Father, serve with pure joy.

CHAPTER 6

And Gave Himself Up For Her

*If we are going to race, fight, or struggle
[in marriage] let it be for who can be the
quickest to be the most humble.*

—Pastor Curtis Meyers

THIS CHAPTER IS ONE THAT hurts the most to write. As a person who has battled all of his life against pride, I am writing myself into an accountability corner. If you are like me, my hasty and selfish opinions have gotten me into trouble more than once. Selfishness undermines the pillars of any successful marriage. They can start them, and mask or suppress their tendencies for a while. Still; without submission to the Holy Spirit, your attempts lead you to your own self-righteousness, making it impossible to have a good, Christ-centered marriage. Jesus' was led to the wilderness to be tempted because he was submitting to the will of God. He was able to keep his focus, not on himself, but on the purposes of God.

A lack of submission can most readily be observed in the way that a husband and wife speak to each other. At some points, you may even be able to see the tension played out in front of you. As noticeable as it may be, because submission is not gender specific, both are in the wrong. A husband has to submit to God first before his wife can even think about submitting. Then, and only then, can the wife submit to her husband as unto God in all things. The Bible is clear, "you cannot serve two masters. You have to love one and hate the other" (Matthew 6:24, KJV). In context, the verse speaks about money and yet it causes us to reveal intent is wherever your heart is, your treasure, is what you serve. As a caution, if you elevate your wife to god-like status, you could be placing them on the level of a deity. God is clear about how jealous He is for that spot in your heart. We are to serve our wives through our service and devotion to Christ's pattern given in His Word. Our sacrifice and submission should not be done in pride; it must be a reflection of Christ's work for his church.

In the Screwtape Letters by C.S. Lewis the main character focuses on how pride is used as a vice. To set the scene, 'Uncle Screwtape', a senior devil, is encouraging his nephew Wormwood, a younger devil, in the ways of our enemy. In the story the enemy is God. He offers suggestions on how to use pride in one's humility to help lose sight of the fact that sacrifice, if not done selflessly, is rooted in pride.

"Your patient has become humble; have you drawn his attention to the fact? All virtues are less formidable to us once the man is aware that he has them, but this is especially true of humility. Catch him at the moment when he is really poor in spirit and smuggle into his mind the gratifying reflection, "by Jove! I'm being humble," and almost immediately pride — pride at his own humility — will appear. If he awakes to the danger and tries to smother this new form of pride, make him proud of his attempt — and so on, through as many stages as you please. But don't try this too long..." Uncle Screwtape pulls at the idea that submission is a daily or moment-by-moment requirement. 1 Corinthians 10:12 (AMP) "Therefore let the one who thinks he stands firm [immune to temptation, being overconfident and self-righteous], take care that he does not fall [into sin and condemnation]."

You cannot be filled to the brim with your own arrogance and see your spouse appropriately. Similarly, you cannot hope to know your wife atop the fortress of solitude created by pride. When the conversation of humbling oneself comes up it offends you. How do you know if you are offended? You may ask, but it is easy; you defend everything in yourself you qualify as good. This occurs even when you are knowingly at fault and that is pride.

A quick story to serve as an example:

Our dating life was tumultuous; we argued over most things and could not understand what was happening to our love story. We often settled arguments with, "we're just two very different people; but that settled nothing. Prior to marriage, I was resolute in not putting a great deal of information about our dating online, self-identifying as a "private person." Shortly after marriage, we revisited that discussion. My wife has her own social media presence and following that she cultivated over years of operating in her purpose. Many follow her who need motivation to pursue, persevere, and ultimately accept their own identity in Christ. Due to this, every event and I mean every event had a photo, caption, and a flurry of comments. She wanted me to join her and to become a dual-threat over social media. We would be King and Queen Carter, or simply, THE Carters. She was ready to jump into conferences, speaking engagements; my head was spinning. I was reluctant, not desiring the spotlight. I did not even like my picture taken unless I was being silly or it was a candid shot. At the root was a deep lack of confidence in my own appearance and had little to do with her.

I vehemently protected my social media accounts from being, what I perceived as, an extension of hers. I even went as far to say,

"My social media is not a billboard for you to push your product. I have a right to not post your stuff if I choose." Some of you may agree that I was well within my right. From one perspective, yes, but there was more to it than that.

I wanted to protect what was mine. I wanted my standard of privacy to be our standard, but that isn't she is and I knew it and at the end of the cycle of argument she would say, "we just don't work well together." It would be easy to dismiss this because social media may not be that important to you but there were bigger issues at stake. My rights as an individual operator was under threat and I was not okay.

More recently my wife and I we're looking to buy a new house. Though we had great hopes that we would find something quickly, the market was very slow for our price point. My wife believed that God would not release us to go into our own home if we did not take care of what we have now. As a result of this, we began fixing up our townhome as if it was going on the market next month. I was putting together blinds, dressers, backsplashes, and so much more. But, the greatest project was our backyard area. My wife wanted bricks laid, a canopy over top, and furniture assembled. Admittedly I approached this project very timidly siding every reason that I could as to why we should not spend the money on this project. Dragging my feet for a very long time, I was hoping and praying that we would have a new house before lacing up any work boots.

The time came where, in frustration my wife and I, disagreed about how we should do this and in our trip to Home Depot, we looked for the sales associate to mediate our dysfunction. I wanted them to see that I was right and so did she; this project was never going to get done like this. I used every excuse I could think of and had great logic to back up each one, or so I thought. One night after another round of questions as to when the project would be finished,

I decided to go outside to lay more bricks. It wasn't until the next day that the true intent of this project came out in a way that I could finally hear. She said, "The reason why I want the outside finished is because I need a space to create and relax. That space would give me so much calm and peace." The decision in front of me was to hold my position or to give up my desire for temporary peace for the greater good. Five days later the project was finished.

Do you see what happened here? My resistance elongated the process but when I gave of myself so that she could have a place to rest, we both found peace. I cannot tell you how hard it was to lay the brick, assemble furniture pieces and a canopy was but I was exhausted after it all. I fought so hard for so long because all I wanted as my time—my quiet space—my ability to be my own boss. I wasn't battling her. I was in a battle with my own selfishness.

To give a definition of selfishness; it is the pursuit of your standards, desires, and will at the expense of another person. I would venture even further to say it is selfishness that is wrapped in a heart that covets and laments older seasons of singleness. In fact, if you examine selfish intentions the root thought is, "I never had these problems before I met you." That mind is not like Christ. It exists outside of God's covenant and with that mind you supplant your vows. Remember it's not the large sins or actions that kill us, it is the small foxes that destroy vineyards; that is to say, they threaten all relationships.

A married man has to be faithful in his actions but also intentional in his thought life. Your old life is done, gone, finished, over with, passed, never to return, nunquam postea! So, then we approach this section of the scripture without timidity and with a singleness of heart. "He gave—himself—up—for her" those are bone-chilling words for any husband. There is much talk about what husbands should receive or rather what he deserves in carrying the title of the husband. The often quoted and abused "wives honor your husbands" (1 Peter 3:1 and Ephesians 5:33, KJV) we want ours first, before doing what we were commanded to do. In order to receive the reward of honor from our wives we must apply a principle I call 'The principle of the first partaker' according to 2 Timothy 2:6 (KJV), "the husbandman that laboureth must be first partaker of the fruits."

Looking at Jesus as our example, we see so many admirable characteristics. Jesus says he only did what he saw the Father do first (John 5:19, KJV). Therefore, if we are truly submitted to God, we should be first partakers. The first to show generosity in the family should be the husband. The first to be selfless should be the husband. The first to show respect should be the husband. The first to live humbly should be the husband. Many of these attributes are placed on the wife because, naturally, she carries a closer relationship with her emotions and empathy whereas most men do not. How can this be and should it continue? You were not made to be a taker but a giver. If you can give seed, prioritize provision, give correction, then you should also be able to give an apology. You are the leader of the home, by God's standard in covenant partnership with your wife.

She may know how to do all of those things better than you, but it does not take away from the fact that you should be doing it first and to the best of your ability. Keep in mind that the result of your submission is unity. The result of your unity is peace. The result of your peace is prosperity. The Apostle John says this, "Beloved, I wish above all things that thou mayest prosper and be in health, even as thy soul prospereth." (3 John 2:2, KJV).

CHAPTER 7

"I Go To Prepare a Place for You"

If God doesn't build the house, the builders
only build shacks. If God doesn't guard the
city the night watchman might as well nap.

—Psalm 127:1 (MSG)

BEING A HUSBAND IS AS much about execution as it is about preparation. For those of you reading this who are not married yet, there is still time to prepare. For those who are married, you may notice compromised areas in your foundation, which is not a terribly uncommon realization.

According to the Jewish Encyclopedia, husbands in ancient Israel had a huge responsibility prior to marriage. It says, "The husband's duty to furnish (to provide clothing for) his wife is also regulated by his station (occupation) and by local custom. He is [obligated] to provide a home, which must be suitably furnished in accordance with his position and custom. Besides furnishing her with the proper garments suited to the seasons of the year, and with new shoes for each holy day, he must also provide her with bedding and with kitchen utensils. She must also be supplied with ornaments and perfumes, if such is the custom. If he is unable to provide his wife with a suitable outfit, he is compelled to divorce her (Ket. 64b; "Yad," l.c. xiii.

1-11; Eben ha-'Ezer, 73)." When I read this to my wife, without hesitation she said, "I want a do over." I told her she would receive a reversible onesie, a bejeweled headscarf, and socks with toes in them. I continued, "If you're nice to me I might throw in a pair of crocs and a spatula;" that was my final offer.

Suffice it to say, at the time of our wedding I wouldn't have qualified to marry my wife. But Christ, the ultimate gift giver, is more than prepared to do all of that for us. He told his disciples he was going "to prepare a place for you that where I am you might be also (John 14:3, KJV)." That prepared place is not limited to the mansions we have heard about from older saints, it also includes the blessings that come from within the covenant.

You may have already purchased gifts or even a house. Do your best to resist the lure to become materialistic. The prepared place has less to do with what is in the house and more to do with what future you are preparing, this is foundational work. Previously, we dealt with soils and similarly, this has to do with what you are building upon. Jesus told Peter that he would build his church upon a rock able to withstand the furious opposition of the enemy (Matthew 16:18, NIV). What is your house built on and is it able to stand against opposing forces? The level of resistance that comes in the beginning of your marriage is far different from the ones that come later. In the beginning, you may have had to navigate differences of role expectations or familial pressure to be present at all family events. Later you might feel the weight of a health crisis, infidelity or a type of loss. Each situation that you face pokes at the foundation of your relationship which is why building your marriage on the saving work of Christ is imperative. How do you build your marriage on Christ?

"Suppose one of you wants to build a tower. Won't you first sit down and estimate the cost to see if you have enough money to complete it? For if you lay the foundation and are not able to finish it, everyone who sees it will ridicule you by saying, "This person began to build and wasn't able to finish (Luke 14:28-30, NIV)." Jesus points to the fact that when you want to take on a task you have to count the cost. Some may have been under duress to the "marry or burn" theology or unforeseen pregnancy while others may have been measured in their approach. If you are already married, you are probably asking how you can do foundational work again while others may be trying to access the checklist before your wedding day.

Here are a few areas to consider:

Have You Laid the Groundwork for a Financial Future?

I could share with you stories of my missteps and we would all have a good laugh. I thought I knew how to prepare myself financially for marriage. I saved up a small sum of cash and my bills were in good standing; minimum payments on my credit cards were never late. This is not a sufficient example of preparation. A secured financial future from a biblical financial perspective is threefold: destiny, service and legacy. These three areas start with questions. On the subject of destiny, we are being asked, are you preparing your finances to fulfill your God given destiny in measured, informed, prayerfully considered steps? On the subject of service, consider if your heart postured to help others (2 Corinthians 9:7, KJV). Finally, in the realm of legacy, what will be said about the way you used the resource of money? Will your children be positioned with inheritance or left begging? (Proverbs 13:22, KJV).

Your decision to become a husband and the legacy of it will be largely measured in how you laid the foundation of provision. Debt is a stronghold and a household word for many to the extent that we have not ever experienced financial freedom. Our culture teaches more about accruing and managing debt than becoming debt free early in one's life. Contrasted against the 'American Dream' and debt starts to feels more like a ball and chain, than the pursuit of true financial freedom. God wants us to be lenders not borrowers and Paul tells us to owe nothing to any man except for love (Deuteronomy 28:12, Romans 13:8, KJV). While I have never paid a bill in the currency of love, the path to owing no one should be the goal for each of us. Of course, if you are not in a position to meet all of the steps it does not disqualify you from becoming a husband nor bequeath your current position. There remains an opportunity to ask God to help you be a better husband in the area of stewardship. Stewardship is how you manage what you have been given. Stewardship takes different forms ranging from managing the household budget to partnering with your spouse to set spending limits for an agreed upon goal.

Though I consider myself a financial novice, I surround myself with people much smarter than me for guidance. Here are a few quick and easy steps that I have learned to follow to lay a good financial foundation for your financial future. First, teaching yourself how to honor God with your first. Where you stand on tithing is entirely subjective but the principle teaches you to honor God as your head and manage what you have been given. One e-book that I would highly recommend is by Francisco Javier titled *A Comprehensive Guide to Tithing*. Secondly, are you paying your bills with the intention to get rid of them or are you simply managing it? Thirdly, are you putting money away for savings and do you have at least three months of expenses saved? Fourthly, are you giving to the less fortunate? When we give, we invite the blessings of the Lord to come to us in amazingly unexpected ways (Luke 6:38, KJV).

Another tool I highly recommend is enrolling in Dave Ramsey's Financial Peace University and patronizing their YouTube channel as great resources to help you in this area. I have personally benefited from a lot of the knowledge shared and I know that you can too. As a believer, Dave Ramsey speaks Kingdom language and wants everyone, Christian or not, to be debt free and live an amazing life!

Have you laid the groundwork for an emotionally stable home?
An emotionally stable home, as we have already addressed is one built around safety and provision. Safety is necessary for there to be any substantive conversation of faith or future. Emotionally stable does not just mean outward safety for your spouse but also inward safety for you. To cut to the chase, what disturbs your peace, Sir? What keeps you locked in the cycle of emotional bondage that you can't seem to get free? Perhaps you live everyday trying to prove to the parent that left you years ago that you are worthy. Maybe that ex who told you that you would never find another to love you as deeply as they did, has you wondering if you are truly lovable. It could be great anxiety, fear or depression around the idea that you are failing as a husband, father, leader, etc. I can assure you those are lies from the pit of hell.

Whatever fills the meditation in your heart is what will permeate your atmosphere. From there "out of the abundance of the heart the mouth speaks (Luke 6:45, KJV)." Your enemy wants you to agree with the negative emotions so that you can be ensnared by your own words. 1 Corinthians 6:12 (KJV) says, "Everything is permissible for me," but not everything is beneficial. Everything is permissible for me, but I will not be mastered by anything." Are you allowed to have moments of sadness, unsure, wary of the future, in deep thought about the sum total of your life? Absolutely. But dwelling on them, turning them from emotions to character traits makes your home, your body and your mind unstable. When you succumb to the defeating thoughts are you mastered by them. Fight on brothers, fight on. As you contend against the enemy of your peace, do not give any ground to the devil, resist him and he will run away like a coward (James 4:7, NIV). Contend until you are that God is with you, contend until you know that you are covered by God, contend until you are sure that you are an adopted, engrafted, son of God (Romans 8:15, KJV). If you find yourself constantly battling with whether you are worthy, how do you "become"? The direct result of Jesus dying was that he gave us access to become sons and to put on the mind of Christ; access to stability.

James 1:8 (KJV) says a double-minded man is unstable in all of his ways. If you are battling between what and who you are or are not, your home cannot be emotionally stable. Your wife will draw elements of her safety and identity in the marriage from who you are. The example is clearly in front of us. We are Christians (Christ-like) because Christ knew who he was, otherwise we might be Paulians or Platonians or something completely different. Christ was the Son of God and he was sure of that even unto His death on the cross and his triumphant rising.

A great recommendation that changed my life was the book ABBA by Dr. Matthew Stevenson pointed to the genuine heart of Father God. It set me wholly on a path to firmly settling in my identity as a son to the point that for years. It brought healing in some areas and strength to others as I am recovering from an orphan spirit, to a revitalized knowledge of my Father; I will not be shaken. Are you willing to be loved by the father in such ways that would cause deep healing? The journey is not for the faint hearted because you will need to face things about your own father. As you hold ABBA's hand the results are well worth it. Some have never revisited the mishandlings of our past or deeply examined the origin of present thoughts. I am praying for you even now that you would invite the Holy Spirit in so you can be restored to love again, believe again, and have real joy again.

Have You Laid the Groundwork for a Physically Healthy Relationship including in your eating habits?

Some of you reading this could compete in a bodybuilding competition while others could give a greatly inspiring story about your former glory days where you almost went pro. What since then? How are you maintaining your health since the days you could eat 3000 calories in a day and still be hungry? I assume your body has not kept up well with that mentality or that eating regimen. If the lion's share of your healthy habits are memories, sir, I can assure you, that your foundation is a house of cards. We could hold a debate on what a balanced diet is and bombard opposing sides with facts. I think we can all agree that our diets consist of more excess than moderation. For that, we have to look at one word in the scriptures, temperance. Temperance, or self-control, is not limited to not flying off the handle when you are perturbed, it is also being able to tell yourself 'no'. If you cannot say no to a snack, a double fried Oreo, or a drink in excess you are controlled by your desires. Proverbs 25:28 (AMP) says, "Like a city that is broken down and without walls [leaving it unprotected] is a man who has no self-control over his spirit [and sets himself up for trouble]." Without self-control, we invite and allow unnecessary struggles into our lives; this is true in all areas. Self-control is paramount to balance. Sure, we would rather stay in bed for that extra hour or have an extra helping of that hefty plate but will your body thank you or punish you? You could skip the gym today and just double session tomorrow until something else comes up. By now, you are backed up about 56 sessions, sir.

Jesus' exercise and dietary regimen was nothing like ours today. In scripture, we don't see him smoking, drinking liquor, training to compete in athletic events or even having a dietitian. What we do know is he walked everywhere, which means that he was used to getting his daily steps in! It was not a daily goal for a New Year's resolution; it was a lifestyle. In that time, he learned self-control because no one can be that active without taking care of themselves. In his 40 day fast, He mastered the ability to deny His body the easy way out. That easy way usually has short life expectancy. Ultimately, you can eat and work out as much or as little as you would like at the cost of your own life. Some people have chosen a more plant-based diet to give themselves the best chance to live long lives. Please, consider your own family history and weigh the effects of any and all imbalance in diet or exercise. Your health decisions cannot be swayed in a sentence in a book but what are you doing today to live for tomorrow? Your body being a temple for which you are responsible for should make the difference. You do not want the temple's abilities cut short on the account that you could not control your yeses and your nos. As a matter of fact, in the spirit of an old coach or gym teacher, go take a lap and drink some water!

Have you laid the groundwork for a spiritually healthy family through a personal relationship with God in prayer?
Do you lead your wife spiritually or are you being dragged like a lifeless article of clothing? Does she see you honoring, serving and worshipping God? This is one area that we can undeniably agree that Jesus was the best. Jesus prayed for the church for their minds, hearts, destinies, weaknesses and more. Do you think that was the icing on the cake or was it foundational work? The scripture points to the latter (Luke 22:32, KJV) and in all of the transitions that the church would go through, it was that prayer for their faith in the midst of aggressive opposition that shows his husband-hood.

Here again we visit 'The principle of the first partaker'. I believe a husband should be the first one awake; praying, worshipping, and listening for what God is saying and doing. As difficult as that may be, the analogy that I think of is; would you run a marathon if it meant saving your family? Many of you would run further. Prayer is the marathon that has high moments and low moments. Moments where you hear God clearly, feel his direction and other moments where you wonder if God can even see your situation, feel your frustration, or even care. The answers found in focused prayer and it translates into how you lead your family. Dr. Joe Martin on The Real Men Connect podcast grounded me when he often discussed his devotion time and what answers he received from God. It was as if the words he received were constant answers with profound impact. Too many men do not have a legacy of praying, worshipping, or being full of the zeal of the Lord. This cycle must be broken. It can only be done by men who want God for more than his blessings but for the salvation of everyone connected to him.

With that goal in mind, I set out on a journey of prayer and consistency. This would be my crucible. I would force myself awake just to sit with God—hearing only the HVAC unit turn on and off and feel like I was not heard. Until one day, God showed me that if I could quiet my thoughts through focusing on the Word, I would amplify His voice. I began praying the scriptures, taking my frustrations to God in prayer and through journaling. I called my brother often on my way to work and discussed faith, family, finances, fears, and failures capped it all. When God was the pinnacle of my desire, what flowed was the alignment I needed all along.

Men, prayer doesn't just change situations, it changes you. I have said all of this to say that when you are laying the groundwork for a God-led marriage, you are asking to be put on the potter's wheel and changed. Of all the groundwork to be done this is the one that will bring the most strength, add value to your relationship and create a legacy in your home of which you are the catalyst.

Have you laid the groundwork for healthy relationships together and separately?

It is vitally important that you each have your own friends and friends that you share as a couple. As a man, you need connection and camaraderie. That is not a license to be single when you are around them. Foundationally, you need to establish boundaries with your guy friends that your marriage is the most important human to human relationship that you have. The establishment of clear boundaries looks like making a distinction between your single life and married life. That means staying out all night with your single friends; unsafe. Entertaining random "hey big head" or "I was just thinking about you" messages on social media; dangerous. Focusing conversations on old flames allows a foothold for your enemy to wreak havoc in your relationship. Some single friends will not understand your need for these boundaries but perhaps, you showing them proper balance can be a powerful witnessing tool. The people who cannot respect the boundaries need to be first on the chopping block.

Marriage can be fun when you journey through it with like-minded individuals. As a couple it is so important to have married, committed, couple friends. If those friends are also believers you can count that as an even bigger blessing. Those relationships can help to sustain your marriage and your salvation by creating a shared space for you all to talk openly and honestly about anything inside or outside of your marriage. Subjects can range from finances to children to the bedroom and not miss a beat. God gave us fellowship to enjoy and grow in. If you've been burned by past attempts to find 'couples friends' be patient and enjoy your spouse until the opportunity arises. The time spent with them or your partner is time well spent.

Leave and Cleave

I won't beat around this bush; I've been anxiously waiting to get this piece out. We have to deal with the relational ties that come into the marriage with us. This is so deeply foundational that Adam, the first man, says after seeing Eve for the first time, "Therefore shall a man leave his mother and father and cleave unto his wife (Genesis 2:24, KJV)." Those parental relations can keep us in a boyish state. Paul says when he was a boy, he did child-like things and had child-like thoughts but when he became a man, he put away those childish desires, thoughts, and behaviors (1 Corinthians 13:11, NIV). The main issue with leave and cleave, plainly put, is that we as men are allowed a return to a place where our ego is stroked. It's a codependent relationship with our parents where they need us to be children to relive their happiest moments and we need to feel coddled, unjudged, and devoid of responsibility. God desired and designed us to depart from the needs of adolescence into maturity in marriage (Genesis 2:24, KJV).

My first semester at university I saw something downright appalling. On a Friday morning, I went to do my laundry because I didn't have classes. I thought the laundry room would be empty because most of my classmates were in class. When I walked in, I saw a mother standing there washing and folding clothes. I was puzzled because weren't we in college? Wasn't this supposed to be the place where parents would not be involved with our lives? Surely, this student was injured or incapacitated and she was just helping him out, right? Then he came down and asked if she was done with his clothes yet. I wouldn't have believed it if I didn't see it with my own eyes. However, we were recently emancipated from our parents and on the path to adulthood I couldn't help but wonder how long his mom had been doing his laundry and how much longer she would continue. In my adolescent years, in between complaining and sports, I believed that chores would prepare me to be on my own. The process of leaving and cleaving had begun. What was it that he needed from his mom at this point in his life? Wasn't this the 'adulthood' we all were so anxiously awaiting?

I don't know what became of that young man or if he ever learned to do his own laundry but he and his mom had an agreement about him remaining coddled. Without the relationship maturing his mother would have unbridled access to him. This would not go over well if he were to marry a woman who felt that doing that was her responsibility, or worse, his own responsibility. The amount of "momma's boys" that are either self-proclaimed and closeted cannot be understated. The severity of this membership ranges from your mother still offering to clean up your house to having the freedom of speech and opinion to wield as a weapon against your wife. Brothers, these things ought not be so.

The notion of leaving and cleaving is present in every ecological system known to man. No organism lives and dies with its parents, we are not made to do so. That being said, it is unjustifiable and a biblical violation to have your parents as the third wheel of your marriage in any capacity. I know you are thinking "that is my mom/dad and people need to understand their sacrifices all of these years." Your wife cannot be your wife as long as your mother is your wife. To be blunt, "leave and cleave" protects against the division you will experience within yourself in moments of conflict between the two mammoth personalities and allegiances. When Jesus was on the cross, taking his final breaths he knew that the joy set before him was his bride and so he did what a good son should, charged the care of his mother as his primary responsibility to another. You see, Christ could not fully embrace his bride while attempting to embrace his mother. Why can't the two coexist? Can they just get along? The mother and the wife are, at best synonymous, and at worst synonymous. Yes! You read that correctly. Both are passionate caretakers, dutiful protectors, and serial investors, resourceful with impeccable memory. Both are willing to go to war for the man they love. Your responsibility in the matter is to create and inform all parties of the boundaries by which you will operate, respectfully. Not being part or parcel to badmouthing the other in your presence, not having side conversations in exclusion of your wife, not prioritizing your mother's needs without discussing how it impacts your family with your wife, not neglecting your mother's needs because of your wife and those are just a few examples. The tightrope you walk is an arduous one. The right balance shows compassion and fairness to both parties. You may not get this right the first fifty times but when you do, the peace that flows from it will be tangible.

CHAPTER 8

The Called, Go

Men do not read the Bible, but they read us,- do let us give them a good version of the Scripture in our lives. They will not study our doctrinal opinions, but they will examine our practical examples; and if we are not what we ought to be, we wound the Savior afresh, stab at the heart of his gospel, and impede the progress of His kingdom.

—Charles Spurgeon

SINCE THE TIME YOU WERE in kindergarten you have been asked one question on every level and in every educational space, "what do you want to be when you grow up?" For whatever reason we reached for occupations that we regarded highly even if we didn't know anyone in that field. Police officers, doctors, lawyers, teachers, athletes topped the list every year. As we grew older, the conversation became less about employment and more about one's life purpose. Who are we and what are we meant to do? For some, this answer came suddenly when finding a passion for an industry or occupation. For others, you journeyed through a labyrinth of life experiences and found purpose unexpectedly. No matter how you found your purpose, it was accompanied by a deep sense of knowing, this is what I am called to do. Perhaps, even what you were created to be.

When we look at the lives of the apostles, they were in full functioning occupations when Jesus approached them. For some, he changed their name on the spot, while for others, he changed their desire by offering a sense of purpose and a calling. Even when they attempted to return to regular work after Christ's death, they longed for purpose. Christ's death was not the only reason they continued to martyrdom. It was the profound sense of knowing that the sum total of their lives was in joyful service to God. Similar to the apostles, husbands are called from a life filled with concern for making your name great to making His name great. You have a call on your life. Understanding what you were called to do is simple and if you have never searched for it, I will give you the shortened version. Your purpose in life is to make God's love evident, his image permanent, salvation accessible, and his glory impermeable. The various tools that you have at your disposal through personality, character, talents and spiritual gifts are how you achieve life's purpose.

This is summed up beautifully in Romans 8:28 (KJV), "For we know that all things work together for the good of them that are the called according to His purpose." All things can and will work together when you place Christ and the purpose of God for your life as priority and let everything flow from that place. When we pollute the purpose and misappropriate our calling, downgrading it to an area where we are simply talented, we lose the scope of Christ's work. As a husband, you have been promoted to a higher calling, the promotion of the covenant to the world.

Fortunately, that call doesn't shift or eclipse the calling you might have been following in your single season; it's the same! You are more than equipped for the job as you follow Christ and here is why. A husband must be a "jack of all trades" to lead his family. He must be skilled in checking off honey-do lists, masterful in navigation and most importantly, able to hold five-to-ten-pound purses while she "tries on a few things." You can do all of those things no problem, right? I'm mostly kidding. Husbands have a heavy load to carry because, like a Special Forces operator, they need to be ready to meet the objective in various ways. Even so, we have the five-fold ministry offices given to the church (Ephesians 4:11-16, KJV) from Christ, which are Apostle, Prophet, Evangelist, Pastor, Teacher. Oddly enough, 'husband' is not listed. Jesus himself operated in all five and released them to his Apostles. I want to show you how each of you can operate in these offices within the context of being a husband. This is not a license to change your Facebook name or business cards to World Evangelist Overseer Prophet so and so.

As an Apostle, you're sent to stir your wife in her desire to go after her full God given potential, setting an order for how you will lead a Godly marriage together. As Prophet, you reveal God's heart, thoughts, and intentions to her through your words and actions. You encourage her future in the ways of God and in marriage. This is not some sycophantic plot; rather, it is grounded in the Word of God. As an Evangelist, you take the heart of God for a covenant relationship with Him and live a life that invites others to learn and serve God like you. As Pastor, you lead your family with a shepherd's heart: selflessly, watchfully, and patiently. Finally, as Teacher you instruct the family in the ways of God while leading them to develop a hunger for learning and applying the Word. If that sounds like Christ Jesus then it sounds like a good husband. It is normal for men to be strong in one or two areas while dragging the others lifelessly behind them by reason of not knowing how to use them. If you find yourself unsure of how to do it or are lacking understanding, you can ask God for wisdom and he will give it to you (James 1:5, KJV). Each of those offices can function as individual leaders within the church body. You must be willing to lead your wife for her edification or improvement towards unity, maturity, and stability.

Jesus himself said, "many are called, few are chosen." As men, some in our friend groups want to be married, possessing even a deeper desire to have a family but do not want to give up the no-madic dating life. At the present, they qualify as part of "the called". They would be in the boat next to the disciples fishing, hearing the master call for them, but not willing to answer. You, the chosen, are called to be an example in the world of Christ's husbandry to the church. He is a joyful lover, present friend, a gracious giver, and devoted partner. The Apostle Paul urges us to "walk worthy of the vocation wherewith we were called with all lowliness and meekness, forbearing one another in love; Endeavoring to keep the unity of the Spirit in the bond of peace (Ephesians 4:1-3, KJV)."

Go

To look at the life of Christ and his ministry we hold his experi-ence here on earth in high regard. After his resurrection, He spent 40 days with his disciples instructing them. When that was over, He challenged them to go into all of the world making disciples. Today we know it as The Great Commission. Not just some of us, but all of us are being charged to mobilize and evangelize with our lives. Bishop Veron Ashe once said, "God never commanded us to witness, he commanded us to be witnesses. We come and go to church but we don't be church [sic]." He continued, "There has to be a point in our lives where we have to stop telling people what to do and become so evident, that they will see it evidenced in our lives." In most of the healings that Jesus performed, he didn't add the person to the roster of the apostles. He told them to go and show themselves and be the example of what God can do. The same should be said for our marriage. Many of you have harrowing stories of how you and your spouse overcame because you were open to the leading and healing hands of the Father. Yet, when was the last time someone looked at your marriage and saw the example of Christ? They might not be able to put a finger on it so instead they try to describe what they see. Words like, connected, in-sync, good vibes, or "wanting a love like yours." That should excite and humble you at the same time. When asked how you got to this point, the correct and appropriate response is pointing them to the relationship you have with God. The incorrect response is to point to your own efforts as the meter of your success.

The spirit in Christ's parting words was to live the life that points men and women back to relationship with Christ. Notably, the disciples did not take much initiative after The Ascension. They were like those of us who, after the wedding festivities concluded, were stuck, not knowing where to go nor what to do. In front of us were two tasks, first, the enormous responsibility to lead our wives. The other responsibility was to mirror Jesus' covenantal relationship with the church in our own marriages. Honestly, who is watching you? I can tell you who, those looking for hope that love is real, that there are good men who still believe in family and its values, to those looking to follow God's will for marriage and the race to submission from the husband first, and then the wife. You are called to go and show the world that Christ still has a burning passion for his bride, the church.

Don't Go Alone

You cannot and should not go at this task individually. Read that again. One more time for the sake of posterity. The narrative that men don't need anyone to be "good" is a lie. As Satan would have it, it's one of those seeds planted early in life that keep many of us prisoners to our own selfishness and pride. You must avoid the bait to attempt marriage alone at all costs. Most importantly, you should not look for community only when things are bad, by then it may be too late. Consistency is key with your circle whether that is a men's group or trusted friends because without it, you will most certainly fall. How do I know? It's much harder to fall flat when you walk with people who are keyed into your wellbeing. Stumbling is part of our sinful nature which we were born into, but a fall is the direct consequence of being lured away by your own lust (James 1:14, KJV). That is why Ecclesiastes 4:10 (KJV) exists to help you understand that when you walk with someone, even if you fall, there is someone to lift you up. But, if you fall alone, you are endangered by staying there much longer. Therefore, to avoid unnecessary pitfalls, your community has to be made up of men who are looking to live in a committed and selfless marriage just like you. Within that community, you need an array of men from the old to the young, the polished to the work in progress, and even the believer and the unbeliever. Every man you select needs to value transparency, demand accountability, prioritize honor, and promote holistic wellness. Above all of these, they must be converted men and not simply in the religious sense. Jesus tells his friends that when Satan desired to have one of them, He "prayed that his faith would fail him not" then followed with, "when you are converted, strengthen your brethren (Luke 22:32, KJV)." I've taken this to mean that after you have come through the trial of your faith, your responsibility is not to boast in your triumph but to humble yourself to encourage your brothers.

Men with these attributes allow you to chase purpose knowing they have your back. As an added bonus, they won't allow you to disrespect your wife even when you are angry, consent to you compromising your salvation, be threatened by your success, or even allow you to stay weighted with heavy negative emotions. If they fit the bill, those men want to see you thriving. You need to make every effort to normalize picking up the phone, speaking with them and setting time to get together.

Why do you need this community? Well, I know that sometimes you just need a break. I won't tell your wife if you don't tell mine. This is not to be taken as a break from responsibility but a break from isolation. Yes, even though your wife is your best friend, you can still feel isolated from your community. You cannot earnestly go after all that God wants for you, your marriage, and your family as a lone ranger. If the Son of Man journeyed with twelve men and countless other unnamed followers do you honestly believe that you can accomplish being a good husband without community? Jesus never sent disciples out individually, and this continued throughout the New Testament because safer and more valuable to the spread of Christianity. I implore you to move beyond finding men who are willing to tell unfruitful stories about their wives and move into a community that builds each other in faith, in value, in purpose and in their marriage.

A Final Word

Jesus is undeniably the highest mark that we should aim to replicate. He is among other things, selfless, loving and compassionate. While we may not achieve even half of what He did for His bride, we are tasked with keeping a singular focus like the Apostle Paul in Philippians 3:13 (KJV). There Paul says, "Brethren, I count not myself to have apprehended; but this one thing I do, forgetting those things which are behind, and reaching forth unto those things which are before, I press toward the mark for the prize of the high calling of God in Christ Jesus." This walk to be like Christ has to be a daily pursuit. Nothing about being a husband is as glamorous as the sacrifice of the cross. We have to die to what we want individually and fervently seek what Christ wants for our marriage. I challenge each of you who read this book to turn off the game, stop the scroll and keenly listen to what God wants to say to you. He wants to teach you to love your wife like He does and show you what it means to be in a covenant relationship. He wants you to rest in Him and not be anxious for any reason. He wants to get the glory out of your life, your valleys and your victories.

When the Bible says that we should first examine ourselves before taking the Lord's Supper, that level of introspection isn't limited to the ritual. Very often, we should be doing a heart check with the Master Architect to ensure that we are in His will for our marriage. When we don't get it right concerning our wives, He can show us how to get back on track. When we get it right, how to celebrate the victory and apply the testimonies. I believe that you can and will see an improvement in your marriage because you aren't following my words as your blueprint. You're following the heart of God and the Mind of Christ and that means you have the license to be a new creature. "Therefore, if any man be in Christ, he is a new creature: old things are passed away; behold, all things are become new (2 Corinthians 5:17, KJV)." Let the old ways of being a husband go, let them die, now! Don't go at this alone or even with friends who only understand based on intellect alone. Submit yourselves to God and he will exalt you in your time (1 Peter 5:6, NIV).

Finally, I leave you with a familiar Pauline prayer "I pray that out of his glorious riches, he may strengthen you with power through his Spirit in your inner being, so that Christ may dwell in your hearts through faith. And I pray that you, being rooted and established in love, may have power, together with all the Lord's holy people, to grasp how wide and long and high and deep the love of Christ is, and to know this love that surpasses knowledge—that you may be filled to the measure of all the fullness of God. Now to him who is able to do immeasurably more than all we ask or imagine, according to his power that is at work within us, to him be glory in the church and in Christ Jesus throughout all generations, for ever and ever! Amen (Ephesians 3:17-20, KJV)."

—Blessings

Acknowledgements

THANK YOU TO MY LORD and Savior Jesus Christ for the blueprints to follow without which marriage would be impossible. To the love of my life, my wife, Carmella, as I learn and grow, you lovingly support and challenge me in all areas. I could not ask for a better partner in this journey. I love you. To my parents Derrick and Wilma for your loving guidance. A huge thanks to my brothers and friends who read the innumerable edits, entertained the conversations and never charged me. To my editor who worked tirelessly to help craft a work I can be proud of, thank you.

Made in the USA
Columbia, SC
27 February 2021